Your Life,
Your Story

Books written by Cherry Gilchrist include:

The Soul of Russia: Magical Traditions in an Enchanted Landscape

Everyday Alchemy

The Elements of Alchemy

Stories from the Silk Road

The Circle of Nine: The Feminine Psyche Revealed

Love Begins at 40: A Guide to Starting Over (with Lara Owen)

A Calendar of Festivals

The Tree of Life Oracle

Life in Britain in the 1930s

Sun-Day, Moon-Day: How the Week Was Made

And contributions to:

Sky and Psyche

Tales from the Tarot

World Atlas of Divination

Your Life, Your Story

Writing your life story for family and friends

CHERRY GILCHRIST

piatkus

PIATKUS

First published in Great Britain in 2010 by Piatkus

Copyright © 2010 by Cherry Gilchrist

The moral right of the author has been asserted

A CIP catalogue record for this book
is available from the British Library

ISBN 978-0-7499-4270-0

Text designed by Emma Ashby
Typeset in Swift by M Rules
Printed and bound in Great Britain by
MPG Books, Bodmin, Cornwall

Papers used by Piatkus are natural, renewable and
recyclable products sourced from well-managed forests and certified
in accordance with the rules of the Forest Stewardship Council.

Mixed Sources
Product group from well-managed
forests and other controlled sources
www.fsc.org Cert no. SGS-COC-004081
© 1996 Forest Stewardship Council
FSC

Piatkus
An imprint of
Little, Brown Book Group
100 Victoria Embankment
London EC4Y 0DY

An Hachette UK Company
www.hachette.co.uk

www.piatkus.co.uk

To my husband Robert, who has opened a new chapter of my life story, and to my children Blake and Jessica, who are an essential part of it.

And also in memory of Charles Parker, the renowned BBC radio producer and creator of the Radio Ballads, who inspired me to listen to the songs, stories and views of individual people, and who taught me that no one is ever 'ordinary'.

Contents

Acknowledgements

Many thanks to Michael Kimball, for permitting me to use an example of his ingenious 'Life Stories on a Postcard' (www.michael-kimball. com/blog.php). Also, to publishers Constable & Robinson for kind permission to quote a story from Carmel Reilly's book *The Day My Life Changed*. (Magpie Books imprint edition, London, 2006).

Warm thanks go to my agent Doreen Montgomery, and to editors Denise Dwyer and Anne Lawrance at Piatkus.

Special thanks too go to the students in my summer school classes, who have provided fascinating material from life story writing, and given generous permission to quote from it in this book.

I'd also like to thank the team at Dorothy House Hospice for giving me the wonderful opportunity to help patients with their life stories. Please note that although I have drawn on the remarkable experience of working with these patients, none of their life stories are quoted directly here, as confidentiality remains an essential component of the project.

Finally, my thanks to Derek Blackburn, for supplying me with life story references in psychology and sociology journals.

Introduction

Writing your life story is a unique contribution to the world that only you can make. You have a story to tell – it is a history, a narrative and a biography, and one which you alone know from the inside and are qualified to write. And, despite any modest reservations that you may have about its importance, it will have interest and significance for others in this world, especially your family, your friends and future generations.

How I Came to Life Stories

I was always attracted to the unofficial history behind the kind they taught at school, consisting of lists of kings and queens, dates of battles, treaties and long-ago rebellions. What I wanted to know was *how* people lived, what they wore, and what they ate. At that time, social history was considered an inferior version of 'real' history, and when I asked my teacher why we couldn't study it, she shrugged and said it was no different from the other kind, really. I learnt, in the long run, that she was wrong.

However, in the meantime, I was already drawn like a magnet to the new 'folk' revival, especially to traditional folk songs which had been passed down through the generations. I got into trouble with the headmistress for singing in somewhat dubious folk clubs in the backstreets of Birmingham, when I should have been safely incarcerated at home, revising for exams. But she couldn't stop me, as my parents didn't object. In their innocence, they thought it was a harmless pastime – which it was, pretty much, apart from the underage drinking of a shandy or two and consorting with charming Irish folk singers.

I also joined an influential folk study group, led by the now legendary Charles Parker, BBC producer and inventor of the Radio Ballads. He was highly political, emotional, and passionate about 'the people's' heritage, and while I wasn't interested so much in the politics, I embraced the rest enthusiastically. I helped him to record the songs of Cecilia Costello, an aged lady of Irish stock who not only sang superb and haunting ballads to us, but recounted her memories of the early days in the slums of the Jewellery Quarter. At home, after we had moved to Shropshire, I cycled around with a gigantic tape recorder in a rucksack (no compact versions then), hoping to gather gems of song as they fell from the lips of pure and honest country folk. It didn't quite work out like that, but I enjoyed it all the same. Later, when I went up to Cambridge to study English, I chose to research traditional May Day customs for my dissertation.

Life moved on, and I left university, got married and took up other interests. I gradually moved into writing about astrology, mythology and old traditions of wisdom, something which remains a core subject for me today. I also wrote a number of social history books for schools. For these, I recorded people's memories, long before it was popular to do so. I still have a tape of a dear friend, who could remember his father weeping as his farm horses were requisitioned for the army in the First World War.

Time passed again, and I was busy as a writer, as a singer of early music and the mother of a young family. I still loved the idea of oral history and recording people's memories, but did nothing further about it. Then, in 2004, I bumped into a former neighbour in the supermarket. She told me that she was working for the local hospice, where they had started a project to help terminally ill patients compile a life story or memory box to pass on to their families. They badly needed volunteers.

Thus began an active engagement with the life story – a genre or pathway in its own right, but one which seemed to draw together the different threads of oral culture that had always appealed to me. I helped patients in the hospice to write their narratives and, eventually, I was asked to help devise and deliver a training programme for new volunteers. I was also, by then, teaching life story writing at summer school and on cruise ships.

Additional training came my way in the form of the short British Library oral-history course – a fabulous experience – and an MA course, which included modules on interview practice and technique. I was in my element, recording people's experiences for various projects, including watching eclipses, and conducting an interview with the old lady who, as a child, named the planet Pluto.

All of which brings me to *Your Life, Your Story*, heralding a further stage of my work, and one that is aimed at encouraging you to write your life story, giving you the guidance and techniques that will help you to shape it.

Life Story Choices

There are many different ways in which your story can be written. You'll find a variety of approaches here, from which you can choose the one that suits you best. Along the way, there are suggestions and exercises that will help you to develop your narrative skills, and questions that may prompt you to go further into the recesses of memory and deeper into the core of your life's meaning.

Your life is not a remote topic to be explored with academic detachment, but something that is infinitely precious. The life you have lived defines who you are, and its story encapsulates your human individuality. So in keeping with this, and with the different aims that each of us has, *Your Life, Your Story* provides you with a toolkit for your creation, rather than a set formula to work to. You will find, for instance, that there are options for getting down either a short or a long narrative, and for either concentrating on one period of your life or charting it up as a whole to the present day. Although the focus is on writing, ways of working with photos and visual materials are also explored, so that you can opt to give these pride of place if you wish.

There are also many other exercises throughout the book, which you can try out both to generate material for your life story and to open up imagination and memory. You may wish to explore these before you define which form of life story you will create, as they can reveal new possibilities. Or, if you have already embarked on your project, they are there to provide additional guidance and stimulus as you go along.

The sequence of the chapters in *Your Life, Your Story* moves from practical, first-base considerations, through to the deeper layers of life experience and its meaning. Alongside all of this are examinations of the nature of memory, of family background and of writing style. These will help you to enrich your chosen form of narrative, and you can select from them as you wish. Although you may benefit from working through the book step by step, it is also designed as a resource which you can dip into as needed, or refer back to later in your life story task. The checklist at the end of the book (see p. 187) outlines the main points and techniques covered, to serve as a reminder and a reference point for the various elements to weave into your story.

Working alone or in company

The book is designed so that you can work through it entirely on your own. However, it can also serve as the basis for group work in a Life Story Writing class. Also, for the solo life story writer, there are places indicated where you might choose to do an exercise with a friend, to invite outside appraisal of your writing, or ask your family members for information.

Essential exercises

Although, as I've said, this book does not have to be used as a step-by-step guide, there are two particularly useful exercises which will help to give your task a firm foundation. Setting up a chronology and writing a short 'blueprint' story (covered in Chapters Two and

Four, respectively) will be invaluable to you when constructing your chosen life story form and, regardless of whether or not you try out all the other exercises in this book, I do recommend that you complete these two. They also work well as stand-alone assignments, so that if, for any reason, you go no further with this project, you will still have produced a basic chronicle of your life that can be passed on to others, and which will, in itself, bring a real sense of achievement.

TIPS FOR WORKING WITH THIS BOOK

- Get a sense of the book as a whole before you start your life story in order to grasp how your project may progress, and the depth it can have.

- Read through each new chapter first before trying out the exercises and detailed suggestions it contains.

- Complete the key exercises of constructing a chronology (see p. 21) and a blue print story (p. 70) even if you omit other sections.

- Work methodically on your life story project, but feel free to take certain exercises or guidelines in the book out of sequence if it's more appropriate for your project.

- Give yourself regular breaks, both in daily sessions and after longer periods of work too. This will help to keep you fresh, and to see your writing with a more objective eye when you come back to it.

- Keep the book to hand as a resource to dip into after you've completed your initial work with it.

To conclude, it is my firm belief that all individuals count for something, that everyone has a story to tell and that the telling of that story enriches humanity itself. Good luck with creating yours.

Cherry Gilchrist, 2009
www.cherrygilchrist.co.uk and *www.write4life.co.uk*

CHAPTER ONE

Writing Your Life Story

Working on your life story can be both a life-changing and life-enhancing experience. You may revisit long-ago scenarios and discover their secrets; you may find new perspectives on the past. Emotions ranging from delight to anger may surface, and recollections of the tastes and scents of your old haunts can flood your senses with an incredible intensity, dissolving the years between old memories and the present moment. But writing your life story is much more than just a way of entering the realm of memory again. The act of writing also helps to organise these memories, and to reveal the patterns and storylines running through your life like those in a rich tapestry. And far from being a task that locks you into the past, setting down your life story can bring renewed enthusiasm for your life as it is now, and refresh your hopes for the future.

What is a Life Story?

A life story is the narrative of an individual life history, spanning all or part of the person's lifetime. It is most often written by the person in question, though it can be taken down and written up by a third party. Life stories can also be recorded in spoken, audio form, which some people find an easier or more authentic way to set out their story. Recording the life stories of individuals this way, often for social history projects, is also a method used by various institutions, such as the British Library Sound Archive in the UK and Story Corps in the USA (see Resources, p. 96).

The term life story or 'life book', as it is also known, was apparently first used in the context of children who had been adopted or fostered, and it came into prominence as a therapeutic aid in the 1980s and 90s. The professionals caring for them or helping them to make the transition from one environment to another, realised that these children needed a sense of their history and their roots, and life story work was used to give them back their past. This is an interesting take on the nature of the life story, often thought of as something for older people to tackle when most of their life has already been lived and, as such, it shows just how significant the life story can be at an earlier stage of life.

Some life stories are the accounts of famous people; others, like those documented for archives, may be used to illustrate a certain way of life – those of potters, fishermen, soldiers and farmers are just some that have been chosen in recent years, for instance. However, it is vital to know and understand that the life story does *not* depend upon you being a public celebrity or a valuable relic of a vanishing way of life!

A well-known journalist who worked on a national newspaper, interviewing presidents and premiers, took time out to volunteer as a life story project leader at the hospice where I too volunteered. 'Everyone has a story to tell', he told each new group of patients as he explained the possibilities for recounting their own stories – stories of human endeavour, of joy and loss, triumph and challenge. They were, he said, in no way inferior to those being played out in the pages of the newspapers, and each one was genuine and of vital and unique interest. I noticed how patients would look at him, with both doubt and wonder in their eyes, as he worked at convincing them that the stories they had were indeed worth telling.

In my own work with patients in the hospice and with students on the life story course, the doubts and excuses were repeatedly voiced: 'My life hasn't been eventful'; 'My life story isn't interesting'; 'I haven't done anything, really, with my life'. But after just a little encouragement, fascinating aspects of these 'uninteresting' lives would start to emerge, for example: 'Well, I did once try sheep farming in Australia', or, 'My family was bombed out during the Blitz.'

In my experience, no one's story is ever dull, even though they may need coaxing to relate it. You will almost certainly have achievements to relate, and your memories may indeed enrich knowledge of social history. But the main reason for writing your life story is its value to you, its uniqueness in human terms and its significance to your friends, colleagues and family.

While there is certainly a readership for life stories in the public domain, it's not always in the form we might like. The term 'life story' is also used today in the popular press for what are often lurid 'true life stories', dripping with sex and scandal. Although these are rather different from the kind of accounts suggested in this book, the emphasis on sensational personal narratives does reflect an almost universal hunger to hear other people's stories. 'It's what readers want,' editors will tell you.

In a more sober context, oral history, the genuine memories of so-called ordinary people, has become a strong element in historical studies now. Back in the 1980s, before it was fashionable to do so, I included memories that I had gathered from individuals in my social history books about the First World War and the 1930s, and I treasure the tape recordings that I made at the time, which of course can never be repeated. Although the books are now out of print, they still remain popular on library shelves, and they are a testimony to our desire to know what people really thought and experienced in times gone by.

More recently, in my co-authored book *Love Begins at 40: A Guide to Starting Over*, Lara Owen and I interviewed men and women about their experiences of dating and finding love in midlife and beyond. We were enthralled by their stories, which covered the whole gamut of human emotion, joy and pain, and were deeply impressed by the wisdom which they had distilled from their experiences.

Life story, autobiography and memoir – are they different?

So, is a life story the same as autobiography, or a memoir? Strictly speaking, they are not identical. An autobiography is a full and literary account of a life, written by the person who has experienced it (as opposed to a biography, which is compiled by a third party). It suggests a full-length narrative intended for publication, and it is usually about somebody famous, or someone whose life has been extraordinary. With life stories, on the other hand, it's the voice of the ordinary individual that counts, along with the authentic experience recorded in their narrative, and they are not usually intended for commercial publication.

The memoir is, in many ways, closer to the life story than the autobiography. Memoirs tend to be records of particularly interesting times or events that the writer has lived through, often connecting to periods of political or social importance. They may be intended for publication, though many people do write memoirs without such a specific intention. So the focus with memoirs is on select parts of your life, rather than your whole lifetime, and this is something you can choose to do in your life story; memoirs are almost a kind of scrapbook in which you paste pieces of your life, and scrapbooks can also be a form of narrating your life story.

However, the word memoir again has a literary feel to it, and can sometimes sound rather old-fashioned. It brings to mind exploits of tiger-hunting colonels in India from the time of the British Empire, or recollections of Bloomsbury soirées in the 1920s. I sometimes use the word memoir when describing life story writing, more for variety than anything else, but the ethos of the life story as a term is more up-to-date, vibrant and accessible to all of us than that of the memoir.

'Life writing' is yet another genre that has come to prominence in recent years, and is used particularly in the context of writing courses; it can form part of a degree in creative writing, for instance. It broadly refers to any writing that you do based on your life experience, so this can include autobiography, memoir, life story or work based around a particular episode in your life that you are exploring and analysing. Writing your life story is thus a valid branch of life writing, but they are not synonymous, and life story writing does not indicate an aspiration towards publication and/or becoming 'a writer' in the way that life writing does.

However, there is plenty to be learnt from these other genres, and I'll be showing you some of the ways in which you can use them for inspiration in your own life story. And something that autobiography, life writing and memoirs all include, which can be extremely useful in the life story, are questions, musings and reflections upon events. These can lift the life story from a serviceable account to a narrative of profound interest, so I will be taking this idea further, especially in the latter part of the book, in terms of exploring the meaning and underlying storyline of your life.

Production and Style of the Life Story

We've established that in the philosophy of the life story, each person's narrative is of value, and so, as such, its presentation doesn't have to be long or literary. That's not to say that anything goes, however: a good life story isn't a tedious list of names and dates or a robotic recitation of events, devoid of any personal feeling. Every life story has the potential to be interesting, but care and thought, and a modicum of skill are needed to bring out that potential. So is the use of imagination to bring your narrative to life, and exploration of memory to retrieve genuine details that can be expressed in a fresh and lively way. All of these elements will be covered in *Your Life, Your Story*.

As mentioned already, most life stories are written for a limited and personal audience, and – in the vast majority of cases – to aim at professional publication is simply not realistic. Furthermore, any ambition to get your story into bookshops nationwide could also hinder the way you write it; you would need to study the market carefully, shape the story in a way that you hope publishers might respond to and set yourself daunting literary standards. And the anxieties generated by trying to get it right for a general audience could have a deadening effect on your efforts. It is nearly always better to concentrate on letting *your* voice come through in *your* way, and telling *your* story how *you* want to. There are ways to print and publish your story yourself for private circulation if you wish, and these will be detailed later on (see p. 35).

In the next chapter, we will also look at the different methods of producing and presenting your narrative so that you are aware of the range of options available. However, even on this score, there need be no pressure to turn out a polished project. You may or may not finish it; you might plan to have the finished account ready in a short time, or you may be happy to go on adding to your life story narrative over many years. It is a flexible project that you can adapt to suit your own personal taste.

Who Writes a Life Story?

Writing a life story can be done by people of any age and stage of their life. A ninety-year-old great-grandmother can do it, looking back over her long life, as can a teenager who wants to set down the memories and chronology of his childhood, before later events obscure or blur them. As we have seen, the life story first came into prominence as a tool for children with disrupted family backgrounds, so it's far from being just an older person's interest.

Of course, it would be unrealistic to suggest that absolutely anybody can do it, as impaired memory or health could make it hard. But the vast majority of people are capable of carrying out the project, and for those who find writing difficult, there are other options such as creating a memory box or making an oral recording (see Chapter Two). There are also contexts in which skilled professionals or trained volunteers help people to compile a life book – for instance in the case of adults with learning difficulties, for whom it is a respected and well-used form of therapy, or in hospices such as the one I worked in.

Your Life, Your Story is mainly aimed at those who would like to write their own life stories, but these other non-written options may open up opportunities for those who need to take a different route. If you are one of these people, you may find that you can still try out a number of exercises in the book, so I would encourage you to look through the different chapters and take from them what you need.

This book may also be helpful for those facilitating someone else's story, such as medical practitioners, care workers, those who work with the elderly or people with learning difficulties, plus social and local historians. Each context has its own requirements. When working with life stories at the hospice, for instance, I learnt that time was of the essence; patients didn't usually have the luxury of years or even months more of life to get their story down. This taught me about the need to be flexible; I discovered how adaptable one has to be in these circumstances, and that where someone is keen to tell their story, a way can usually be found to do it.

But in reality, none of us knows exactly how long we've got, so my advice would be not to postpone writing your life story if the project appeals to you. If you feel that you are still too young to set it down as a story, write journals instead. Make notes on your experiences, and save them for later years. And you can start constructing your own archive at any time: all sorts of bits and pieces – the future memorabilia of your life – such as travel tickets, concert programmes, emails, birthday cards and so on will all be useful and fascinating in future years. Most of us in later life regret throwing away so much, so hold on to what you have!

Why Write a Life Story?

Many people would like to leave an account of their lives for their children, grandchildren and generations as yet unborn. They may regret knowing so little about the lives of their own grandparents, and want to remedy that for their own offspring.

But there are often individual reasons too: 'I want to leave a footprint!' said one enthusiastic hospice patient; he threw himself into the project and, fortunately, had enough time to complete a lengthy narrative, which he published himself and gave to friends and well-wishers at an exhibition of his paintings, another pastime that he took up with passion after the diagnosis of his illness. All this gave him an immense sense of achievement, and proved that he could still live fully even when he was, technically speaking, dying.

Sometimes people are prompted by others to write their life story. One woman who joined my summer-school class explained, 'I kept saying to my grandson, "Well, if you only knew what it was like at that time," until he came back with, "For goodness sake then, Gran, write it down!" So that's why I'm here.'

Other reasons may include wanting to record a fascinating period of history for archive projects, feeling the urge to explore and understand your own past, or even to explain to others why your life has taken a particular course. There is nearly always an emotional component which can fire up the process of writing your life story, and provide wonderful fuel to get you going.

Be careful, however, of more dubious incentives, such as the desire to shock or startle others with your revelations or to take revenge on someone who has wronged you in the past. You may indeed encounter such feelings when working on life story material, but they are of limited use in shaping the whole narrative. Sometimes, writing down difficult memories can be a way of working through experiences which left you feeling angry and powerless, but I would recommend keeping the bigger picture in mind, and a more inclusive purpose in charting your life story.

I believe that the main motivation for writing your life story is love. It can be love of life, pure and simple or it might be love of your family, both older and younger generations, and a desire to describe your place in that tree of life. It could be a love of writing itself and of telling a story to which you have unique access. Or it could be love of the work that you've carried out over the years, of the people you've met and the places you've been to, so that your life story will be a celebration of that love. Love is a rewarding and enduring reason for writing your story.

REASONS THAT PEOPLE GIVE FOR WRITING A LIFE STORY

- 'I want to leave a footprint!'

- 'I've had a very interesting life, so I want to record it. I think other people will find it interesting too.'

- 'You don't realise you've lived through another world, that today's children know nothing about.'

- 'Although I'm still only in my thirties, I've had some major life-changing experiences, and writing my life story is part of coming to terms with those.'

- 'I told my son, "It wasn't like that!" He answered, "Well then, write down how it was."'

- 'My grandchildren enjoy the stories that I tell them about my life, so I'm writing it mainly for them.'

- 'I want to get down my memories while they're still fresh in my mind. Who knows what will happen later on?'

Who Reads Life Stories?

Even at the start of your project, it's worth thinking about who is going to read it, as this will shape the way you write to some extent.

The most common recipients of life stories are family and friends, with an emphasis on the younger generation. Even if your children aren't ready to read it straight away (we can be extraordinarily resistant to our parents' memories at certain stages of life), the chances are that they will be some day, and that *their* children definitely will. Friends, colleagues and the network of people with whom you have associated over the years may also be keen to read your story.

You do not need to have just one readership, of course, and I often encourage people to think about depositing their story in history archives or libraries; social history is enormously popular, both for schools and adult readers. Local knowledge is also sought after, and can be illuminated by personal accounts, so that your narrative about Birmingham before the redevelopment in the 1960s, or post-war rural life in the New Forest would be a real gem in the county archive. Family history is also growing in popularity, and your story and the relatives you describe may link in with a bigger family tree, with living descendents who would love to learn this kind of personal detail.

Finally, you may want to keep your story private, and not wish for a readership at all. It's your right to keep it as your own property, to share or not as you choose. You might want to take at least your first steps towards setting out your life story as a solitary activity, to ponder and write freely without any thought of being judged or letting out revelations that you would rather keep to yourself.

With all these possibilities, be prepared for your attitude to your project to change. As you gain confidence in writing your narrative, you may want to open it out to more readers, and plan how to produce or present it in a stylish format. Keep your plans within reasonable bounds, so that they do not become too overwhelming, but allow yourself the joy of knowing that your story is going well, and that you would like others to read it.

CHAPTER TWO

Getting Started

When I was a little girl, I believed that everything I did and said was being recorded by an angel. I thought that at some point, late in my life, or possibly after I died – I was somewhat vague about the details – the angel would be ready and willing to play back any part of my life that I wanted to see again. It would be rather like watching a rerun on TV. My 'recording angel' was not of the judgemental variety, but an obliging individual who would simply let me roll back the film of my life and watch it all over again.

It touches me now to think that a child of eight years old would value life so much that she wanted to keep every detail of it safe and ready for recall. It opens up a few interesting questions too, as to whether everything that happens does, in fact, remain embedded somewhere in a multi-dimensional universe, or in the realms of consciousness. Maybe nothing is ever actually truly lost from our own minds.

But however these imprints of life survive, in everyday terms you have to trigger your own process of recall. And setting down a life story narrative takes personal effort. It is far from being a dull and worthy plod through the annals of individual history though, and, because you have to engage with it, by revisiting memories and experiences and fashioning the account in a lively way, it is a creative endeavour. It can transform the way you think about and respond to life past, present and future. If it were simply a kind of celestial television show, you would merely be a passive viewer. This way, you are actively involved.

So there is no time like the present to get started. This chapter contains three key elements that you will need to create your narrative:

- First, there is an exercise to show you how to get going with short passages; this is known as bubble writing.
- Next, we look at the task of building a chronology, which will act as the backbone of your story.
- Finally, the different formats for a life story are set out, so that you can choose the right one for yours.

Although this chapter is presented with these three elements in sequence, you may find it useful to read through the chapter to start with, then choose which of the three sections to concentrate on first. If the main question in your mind at the moment is, for instance, how to set out your story, then the final section on life story presentation (see pp. 28–38) might be the one to focus on initially.

Bubble Writing

Bubble writing is a quick and enjoyable way of producing snippets of writing or cameo portraits for your project. It can give you confidence and often produces very good writing. It is also 'portable' in that you can choose to do it wherever you are, should you have a spare quarter of an hour to write in. Bubble writing is also fun, another important factor; because working on a life story does involve periods of hard work and concentration as you gather your resources and organise structure and content, it's helpful to offset this with writing sessions that encourage a freer form of self-expression. Creating your life story is, after all, a way of celebrating your life, and so the main writing process is intended to be pleasurable and fulfilling.

The way that bubble writing works is by generating associations, of allowing one thought or memory to lead to another in a relaxed and spontaneous way. It helps to stimulate both the flow of memory and the narrative powers of your writing. So take a deep breath and plunge in – don't be too careful, or take too long over it! Often, the quicker and more naturally you do this, the more lively and entertaining the results are.

The first stage of bubble writing

Have a pen and a few sheets of paper (preferably unlined) at the ready.

Choose a theme from your life history that you can write two or three paragraphs about. For your first attempt at bubble writing, it's best to select a topic that is keenly etched in your memory, but one which is not too complex. A family pet from the past or a person you once knew are reliable themes. For the purposes of this exercise, if you choose a person, it should be someone who has played a cameo role in your life (as you are only going to produce a short piece of writing) and who is no longer a part of it, such as an elderly aunt from your childhood or a colleague you worked with twenty years ago.

Take a few minutes to muse on your theme, but don't write anything yet.

Next, draw a 'bubble' – either a circle or oval – roughly in the centre of the page, and write your chosen theme in it, e.g. 'Tigger', 'Auntie Mabel' or 'Evan the boss'. Draw a short line in any direction from the edge of the bubble, as the fancy takes you, and then draw another bubble at the end of that line. In this second bubble, write the first strong association with your theme that comes to you, e.g. 'mouse hunter', 'sucked strong peppermints' or 'drank beer Friday lunchtimes'. Keep words to a minimum, and don't try to 'craft' them in any way. Your bubble captions only need to make sense to you; it doesn't matter if they sound cryptic to anyone else.

Continue drawing more bubbles in this way, and writing more associations in them, directly connected with your subject. Always attach each new bubble with a line to an existing one. But don't give it too much thought – impulse will naturally lead you from one bubble association to another.

You can extend your line from a second bubble to a third bubble, if your second association naturally leads to a third image or thought, such as from 'mouse hunter' to 'roamed far and wide' for Tigger the cat. Or you can start another line from your original bubble if you want to go off on a new tack, such as 'wore loud ties' for Evan the boss. You can also join up two existing bubbles, start a new spread of lines from your latest bubble, and generally play with your bubbles and your associations as you please!

Keep going until the initial impetus runs out, and you feel as though you've run out of steam. (If you don't, you may have chosen too complex a theme, and it may be best to try again with a simpler one.) There are no firm rules, but, in general, between eight and twenty bubbles will give you enough material to work with. You don't have to include every detail; trust your imagination and intuition to put in what's needed.

Let's take one straightforward example created by Belinda, a student in my summer school class.

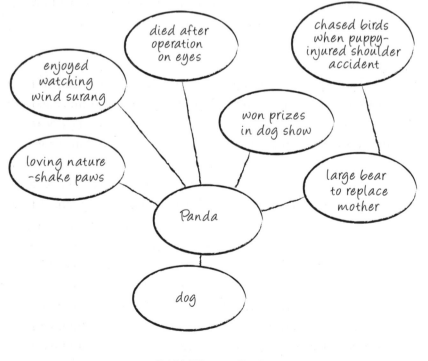

Bubble Writing – 'Panda'

We'll see in a moment how Belinda wrote this up. Her bubble picture is a relatively simple one, but others might extend to several 'generations' of bubbles, and interlink them in a more complex way. When you have tried this out a few times, you will get a sense of which topics generate which kinds of bubble maps, and also an idea of what works best for you.

The second stage of bubble writing

Now you are going to turn your bubble associations into writing. Hopefully, creating the diagram will have generated plenty of energy, and you will, by now, be bursting to tell the story of the pet or person in question. So write a few paragraphs based on your recollections. In some magical way, the exercise of creating the associations usually prepares you for the actual writing as well. You will probably find that ten to fifteen minutes is all you need to get it down on paper. And, although you may find yourself crossing out the odd word here and there, you don't need to edit it into fine prose just yet.

Here is what Belinda wrote:

When our sons, Nick and Robin, were children, we acquired a sweet-natured black and white Tibetan terrier who we called Panda. To make her feel at home, we placed a large teddy bear in her bed, larger than the tiny puppy she was, which she snuggled up to in place of her mother.

She was very lively and chased birds on the common near our house. One day, she chased them on to a nearby road and was knocked down by a car, causing a broken collarbone. She had previously been hard to train, but this injury worked wonders in that respect. When she recovered she was wary of traffic.

She loved watching the family windsurf and would shake paws with anyone she met – indeed a very social dog. Sadly she died after an operation on the eyes which left her blind, and she developed an infection. We all missed her deeply and have not had another dog since.

In a short space, Belinda sketched a vivid picture of the family dog, and covered her essential characteristics, her adventures and the close of her story. You'll notice that she has used all the associations generated in the bubble picture except for one: 'won prizes in dog show'. It's quite normal to omit one or more of the associations simply because it doesn't fit into the narrative flow at this stage; if it's something that you can't bear to leave out, you can probably find a way of weaving it into your writing afterwards.

This exercise often has a knack of bringing out the key events and characteristics of the subject that you choose, without long periods spent frowning as you try desperately to remember them. In bubble writing, because you are not worrying about the narrative to start with, you are likely to produce something fresh and vibrant, with the essentials at the forefront.

One example of a narrative created from bubble associations in a life story class, encapsulates this point in a remarkable way. Simply entitled 'My Eldest Aunt', it made everyone gasp when Julia, its author, read it out. Here is the key section which struck the class so forcefully:

> She was a great pianist (studied in London) and had a grand piano as a wedding present. Her husband, coming home early one day, heard her playing and said in a kindly way, 'Tinkle, tinkle, tinkle'. Belle shut the piano and never opened it again.

The essentials are all there, without elaborate explanations – three sentences that vividly describe a turning point in a woman's life. You can picture the scene, feel the emotions, and reflect on the way that one remark can damage a person's confidence, changing her aspirations for ever.

Taking things further

The basic form of this exercise is now complete, but you can, if you wish, develop it further, by taking the bubble writing you've done and extending, editing or integrating it into a longer narrative. Do keep these accounts within reasonable bounds, though, if you plan to include them in your life story rather than using them as test pieces. A couple of paragraphs on almost any topic from your life can easily be fitted in, but if you've written five pages about the village postman, it may be out of all proportion to the general narrative, and you will either have to consign it to your desk drawer, or work to condense it into a much shorter version.

EDITING YOUR WORK

Be aware that editing your work often takes far longer than writing it in the first place! Don't be afraid to expand, writing in a spontaneous way that will need to be tidied up or trimmed later; this is often the key to authentic and lively writing. But do keep a sense of proportion. A good general rule is to write up to half as much again as you will eventually need. It should then be possible to edit it down to the length required.

Elaine completed a bubble-writing exercise about Snowy the horse, another former family pet. She decided to work on it some more, took it away overnight and brought back the finished version to the summer school class the next day. She had produced an entertaining narrative that we all enjoyed listening to. Here are some extracts from her extended story. Snowy was an ex-show pony, considered to be quiet and mature at the age of thirteen when he was bought for Elaine's four-year-old daughter. However, he turned out to be more of a handful than they had bargained for:

> We soon discovered he was quite a rascal. He was able to escape
> from most fields, a real Houdini . . . A very early-morning tele-
> phone call would herald an 'escape', as neighbours would ring

to say they had seen him hot-footing it past their house, some-times over the A4 – with much screeching of brakes. We thought he must have had nine lives and been related to the cat family. We would all jump in the car, shouting, 'Snowy's out', pull on boots and jeans over pyjamas, grabbing head collars and lead ropes to race round the roads to meet him, flanks heaving as he stood snorting at the gate of his old field again, where he used to live with his fellow ponies.

Snowy also tolerated the family cat jumping on his back for a ride, and on hot days would sometimes wander into the house through the French windows and eat his way through the fruit bowl. Elaine found him there once. He had 'retired to the lounge, his head hanging low, his hind leg resting, as he had a doze. He was just in front of the sofa, and I imagined at any moment he would flop down and sit for all the world like a human resting on a hot day.'

Practising bubble writing

Try out more bubble writing whenever you feel like it, and there should be plenty of themes that you can find which you'd like to include in your life story. Once you are familiar with the exercise, you could extend it across a whole range of topics. However, it is not the only way to write, and I would recommend keeping it as just one of several methods in your repertoire; there will be plenty of other suggestions to try out further on in this book.

Bubble writing probably works best with people, scenes and events which have some colour and meaning for you, but are not the critical, deeply felt elements of your life.

Here are some ideas:

- A house you have lived in
- A special occasion that you celebrated
- A teacher from school
- A journey you made

- A holiday job you took as a student
- A hobby you used to enjoy
- A friend whom you valued
- The different ways you've spent Christmas over the years
- Your first date or first romantic moment

Chronology

A life story is all about time – time lived, time recorded and the sequence of events that define the development of your life. So it's important to give due attention to the business of constructing a chronology for your project. Most people will use a chronological scheme to write a life story; that is, one that progresses through events in the order in which they occurred, more or less. You may sometimes move forwards or backwards in time here and there, but you will still need to have the basic chronology of your life in mind.

Even if you plan to write your story based around themes, rather than linked to a timeline, you will still find it invaluable to map out your chronology first, and to use it as a resource in creating your work. It will give you a structure to work with, and is a great way of checking that nothing important is left out of your life story. It registers the basic pulse of life, the regular beat of year following year, like the rhythm that underlies all music.

The nature of time

Time past is the essence of the life story, so recognising the passing of the years is an inevitable part of working on the narrative. All our most precious memories are embedded in time; and within the march of time we grow as individuals, make discoveries and develop loving relationships. Mostly, we take this passage of time for granted, until, that is, we start recording our life stories, and only then do we recognise just how long ago certain events actually took place, however fresh they may still be in our memory. This can be the case whatever age we're at, whether it's thirty-three or ninety-three.

I recently went to a reunion at a school that I attended between the ages of three and seven – a scarily long time ago. In my mind, I had revisited all the memories of the school many times, but being in that building once again, meeting former pupils (now approaching retirement age), looking at photos and swapping anecdotes, really brought it home to me just how many years have passed since I turned up as a small girl in a grey tunic, trying to hang my coat on a peg that was too high for me to reach.

I recall a dream I had as a young teenager, in which I was several years older, ready to move up into the sixth form. I remember waking up from it in a state of shock: would I really one day be one of those sophisticated older girls gliding like goddesses through the corridors? And would I actually then leave school and start adult life? It was almost unthinkable. Remembering this dream now, I can smile ruefully, but there is also the sobering thought that at some point in the future, I may also look back to this current stage of my life and think of it as a long-ago era.

For everyone, writing a life story does mean facing up to the reality of all the years that are gone, and the uncertainty about how many remain. But if you are prepared for this, and accept it as part of the process, it need not deter you in any way. Many people give up on their life stories because they are unnerved, even disorientated, by confronting the sense of passing years that it evokes. By guiding you through the life story process in a manageable and steady way, *Your Life, Your Story* can help you to move through this potential pitfall. If you stay with the journey, your perspective of time is likely to be enriched, and you will value your life's path even more when you have recorded it.

As my early dream suggests too, there is, in a sense, a part of us which is in some way outside of time, and which doesn't live by the clock. Sometimes called the 'essential self', it is constant from birth to death, and seems to transcend any normal sense of where a person is on their own particular timeline. You may find that writing your life story strengthens your connection with this aspect of your being, and brings you wise insights into the nature of the story that you are recording. Trust that it will take you through to the end. Despite the hardships and trials of life, as Julian of Norwich, a famous fourteenth-century Christian mystic, said: 'All shall be well, and all shall be well, and all manner of thing shall be well.'

MIND DRIFT

While working on your life story, allow yourself pauses for reflection. Take time to let go of time; take a few minutes to step back a little, and let your mind drift gently where it will, backwards and forwards over the years. Let it wander without counting and commentary, and allow yourself simply to experience the ebb and flow of this tide.

Creating your chronology

Here is a way to create your chronology in a way that will work within the context of writing a life story. It is not the only way to map out a chronology, but even if you already have another method in mind, I suggest that you try this one out for a fresh perspective. Once you have tried it, you can always adapt it as you wish.

First of all, you will need to make a chronology template on just one sheet of paper to see how it works. Then you will be able to extend it, possibly over many pages. It's worth thinking about storing it in a separate file or ring binder, so that you can keep it in a manageable and readily accessible form as you work. Although you will be able to complete your basic chronology at this stage, it's something of an ongoing project, and you are likely to add to it as you go along.

LAYOUT

Take a sheet of unlined paper and draw five vertical lines down the page, roughly equally spaced, and with the left-hand one close to the edge of the page. These are going to be your five subject markers, and the dividing lines for your five columns. Allow a little space at the top to write in the headings. If, like me, you are somewhat challenged when it comes to diagrams and geometry, just try it out in rough, and don't worry about being too accurate, at least until you have got the hang of it.

Your central line, the third one along, is going to mark the decades of your life. Write 'Age' above it. Then put '0' at the top of the line. At the bottom of the line, write the age you will be when you enter your next decade. So if you are now aged fifty-four, write '60' at the foot of the column. This gives you '0' at the top and '60' at the bottom of the central line on your page. Now you are going to divide the rest of the line equally to mark the other decades you have lived through. Work out how many divisions you need to make; in the current example, you'll need to put in five more marking points: 10, 20, 30, 40 and 50. You can do this, if you wish, by drawing little dots or cross-hatch lines on the column line. Again, you need not do this mathematically, and can just judge it by eye.

So the section of the line running between 0 and 10 now indicates the first ten years of your life, the second section is your next ten years and so on. The bottom section, from fifty to sixty, is the decade that you are travelling through now. These markers are going to act as your points of reference for age, as you list the events and occurrences in your life. They are the fundamental pulse of your chronology.

You may be thinking that a thirty-year-old is going to have double the amount of space on the page that a sixty-year-old does for each decade. Don't worry about this for now. This is only a trial run, and after you've mapped out your template, you can then create a fuller version, perhaps using one sheet or more per decade, if you prefer. And even though your one-page template may be a condensed version of your chronology, you will still find it useful as a first point of reference.

Now, with the central column relating to age completed, write headings on either side for the other four. These are, from left to right: 'Place', 'Family & Relationships', 'Life Events', 'Work & Study'.

You should now have five column lines named and drawn on

your page, with space between them to write in. This is where you are going to enter the key events and phases of your life, according to the age you were when they took place. Your decade markers on the central column will act as indicators for this.

Let's take an example. Think of the first place that you lived in as an adult. What age were you? Suppose that you were twenty-two and you moved away from your childhood home and went to study in Paris for five years. Put a marker on the Place line at the point which corresponds approximately to twenty-two on your Age line. Then, next to the marker, write 'Paris'. It's as simple as that! And if you want to indicate the extent of the time you spent there, you can draw a little arrow down from Paris to what is, more or less, the twenty-seven-year point on your twenties decade. Or you may find that writing in the place you next moved to will automatically indicate how long you spent in Paris. Take a look at the example below to see what the upper part of the page will now look like.

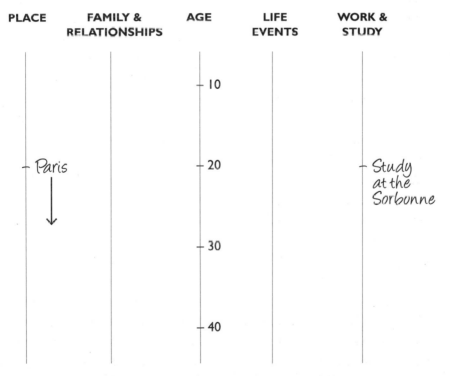

PLACE	FAMILY & RELATIONSHIPS	AGE	LIFE EVENTS	WORK & STUDY
Paris		10		
		20		Study at the Sorbonne
		30		
		40		

An example of how to draw up a basic chronology and enter events

Now, complete your **Place** column, continuing in the same way, starting with the place where you were born, and charting all your moves to the present day. Then fill in the other columns, using the same method. You should be able to enter in overlapping phases, or a cluster of events in the same period without too much difficulty, though as the space on this first chronology template is limited, it's best to be selective; review the key points of your life, and decide which were the most important.

Under **Family & Relationships**, enter both relevant events and phases. Mark up, according to date, events you consider to be significant in terms of births, marriages and deaths and other applicable happenings. You can also indicate as phases who you were living with at a given time (for example your parents during your childhood, a friend for flat-sharing later on) and who you have been involved with in a key relationship, indicating the time span for a marriage or partnership.

Life Events can include anything of major significance, such as accidents, medical issues, major journeys, passing exams and so on. You may occasionally want to duplicate an entry here that you've already included in another column, so that, for instance, 'Moving away from home', 'Divorce' or 'Military service' can stand out prominently.

Work & Study is straightforward, even if you've had a multitude of jobs or tend to follow more than one occupation at a time. Just note when each one started, and, if you like, when they finished, if it isn't a case of a clear sequence from one job to the next. Likewise with education: write down when you started at each school, college and university as relevant. You can also put in markers for any diplomas or extra qualifications that you obtained later on.

EXTENDING THE CHRONOLOGY

Keep hold of this first attempt at a chronology; you may find it useful when you write your blueprint story in Chapter Four. You will almost certainly want to expand it, however, and, as well as allowing more space for each decade of your life, you can include extra subject columns if you like.

Two possible extra headings are 'Travel' and 'World Events'. The first is useful if you have travelled a lot, or taken some significant holidays that you want to tie in with the rest of your life chronology. As for World Events, it's fascinating to write up your life story in the light of these, and to see how your own pattern of life fits into the bigger picture.

Lorna, an elderly friend who we shall meet later on, charts major external events for her life story, and gives prominence to those which have been of special interest to her and her family. For instance, she is enthralled by space travel, so rockets to the moon and space missions feature in her list of events. The freeing of Nelson Mandela from prison was also of enormous significance to her, as she and her late husband grew up in South Africa, but left as young adults to escape the oppressive apartheid regime.

As well as those events which have the greatest personal relevance, there are key moments in history worth mentioning as they affect nearly all of us, such as the death of Princess Diana and the tragedy of 9/11. Later on, you will also see how other events, such as the assassination of President Kennedy, the Silver Jubilee of Queen Elizabeth II and the invasion of Iraq have all played a part in the memories recorded in people's life stories.

You may find it helpful to take a little time to do more research on the history that you've lived through, especially to pinpoint dates of events (see Resources, p. 191, for books that may be useful). If you search on the Internet, typing in a selection of key words such as 'World events dates', or 'World events timeline', you will find plenty of websites with this kind of information (again, see Resources, pp. 195–196).

There may well be other headings that you'd like to use as well, and your chronology will then need to cover a double-page spread. Taking a separate page for each decade can work well, but I suggest that, however much room you give each decade, keep the same amount of available space for each, whether that's an inch or a page. Even if one decade is scantily filled, and the other crammed to bursting, this in itself can be a revelation, seeing how the fat and lean years of life succeed each other. Looking for the busiest, most crowded parts of your chronology can also be an instant guide to choosing which parts of your life you would most like to feature in your life story. In your actual narrative, you can choose to give much more writing space to one phase than another, but in the chronology, keep the beat of time going in a regular way.

INTERNET PRECAUTIONS

All Internet references in this book were correct at the time of writing, but this cannot be guaranteed indefinitely. With this in mind, please follow normal safety guidelines when researching life story topics online.

These include:

- Checking that you have an active anti-virus programme and firewall in operation, according to the advice of your computer technician.

- Proceeding with caution when opening up websites that are new to you on your computer; if a site looks dodgy in any way, exit promptly.

- Either blocking pop-ups, or taking extreme care should they appear on the page; in particular, beware of those inviting you to gamble or apply for a loan and don't click on them at all (not even a 'Cancel' option).

- Never entering your personal details (name, address and so on, let alone financial information) unless you are absolutely confident that a site is bona fide and has a sound reputation.

KEEP YOUR CHRONOLOGY GOING

Once you've got your basic chronology drawn up, you can take your time working on the extended version. You might put aside time specially to do this, or you can just set up your extended pages and simply jot down more happenings as and when you remember them. As you write your life story, you may also be sharing old memories with relatives and friends, who may give you pointers to more events that you want to slot in.

Your chronology is a project in its own right, so cherish and take pride in it. Keep it even when you have finished your life story, as it can be something to enjoy looking through later on and perhaps to pass on to your family. You can also include a condensed version of it at the beginning or end of your narrative.

Timelines and other forms of chronology

You might like to experiment with other forms of chronology, including what is commonly known as the timeline. The timeline, a popular device for showing the timescale of anything from history to business plans, tends to have one horizontal central line marked off in units of time, and along which events are entered. A timeline may give a stronger sense of linear time than the kind of chronology I have suggested above, but I prefer the latter for the purposes of a life story, which is, after all, a complex, many-layered affair, rather than the development of a single event or idea. However, you may find using a timeline to your liking, particularly for charting one event or one kind of theme in your life, and they are fun to try out.

There are many books you can refer to, including history books, that may spark off ideas for timelines. You can also find templates on the Internet (just search 'Timeline template') or you can create them in Microsoft Word and Excel. Microsoft's own search facility has at least one very good template for charting your personal timeline.

Trying out chronologies and timelines can throw up interesting perspectives and insights on your life. You recognise what has been important to you, you see how certain events ran in parallel to each other and, by examining the threads of your past life, you may see how those threads have combined to create the overall pattern and story woven through your lifetime.

How to Present Your Life Story

Choosing a format for your life story is very important, and something that you need to consider early on, as the type of presentation you opt for will define the way that you write and select material. The main options given here are for a written narrative, since writing is the focus of this book. However, there is plenty of scope within these to include visual material too. And just to round out the picture, other methods are explained, such as making a video or voice recording or assembling a memory box. These could be useful, for instance, if you or someone you want to help has limited time or ability to create a written life story.

The categories of life story mentioned are flexible too, and they often overlap with one another, so that there is scope for you to devise your own personal form of presentation from these basic ones. And although choosing a format sooner rather than later is recommended, you may want to leave some room for manoeuvre, so that you could decide later to extend your narrative, for example, or increase the amount of visual material included.

Be realistic right from the start about your time frame. If you are someone who only has a brief window of opportunity to devote to your life story, or you tend to work on a short burst of enthusiasm, then opt for a manageable, small-scale project. If, on the other hand, you don't want to rush to make up your mind, then you could keep format options open until you have written the 'blueprint' story (see Chapter Four). Completing this short version of your life story should give you a much clearer idea of how you would like your main presentation to be.

Tip:
Keep your life story project manageable, to suit you, your personality and your time frame.

Written life story presentations

There are five main ways to present your life story in a form that is chiefly comprised of words, as follows:

1. A typed or handwritten personal narrative of any length.
2. A ring binder with pages added in as you go.
3. A mixture of photographs and/or other memorabilia with written descriptions and narratives woven around them.
4. A ready-made life story book or scrapbook, following a suggested template.
5. A collation of journals, letters or narratives that you have already written over the years.

All of these options (which will be discussed more fully below) may contain visual items too, and indeed, most life stories are all the better for having photographs or illustrations included.

Tip:
Always make provisions for creating copies of your life story. It would be a tragedy if your one sole copy was lost or destroyed! Plan to scan, photocopy, duplicate or print your presentation as you go along.

I. THE TYPED OR HANDWRITTEN ACCOUNT

We'll be exploring the different elements of written accounts throughout this book, so a short description will be enough for now.

As mentioned earlier, a written life story usually progresses chronologically, following events as they unfold. A full life story starts from birth and continues up to the present day. However, it's perfectly acceptable to take a selected slice of your life to form the basis of your narrative – your childhood, for instance, or the years spent at work.

A chronological life story is the easiest to handle in terms of structure, though an alternative is to devote chapters or sections to different aspects of your life – family, work, travels and so on. But this can prove more complex to organise, so if it is going to be of any length, it will require thorough planning in the early stages.

Your life story should be a pleasure, rather than a chore to create. Think carefully before you embark on what you intend to be a full-length life story, as long as a published autobiography, for instance, and resist the temptation to be overambitious. This can be a very demanding project, even for an experienced or professional writer. You may be bursting with memories that you are longing to set down, but a life story has to be selective. It needs structure, as well as content, and it needs to keep the reader's interest, even though it is not aimed at a commercial market.

In general, I would suggest writing the equivalent of 40–100 pages of a book, which would be around 15,000–35,000 words, but less is also fine. If you make a plan based on these parameters, you will probably find that the material and memories shape themselves accordingly. And the exercises and techniques in this book will also help you to select and structure your work.

2. RING-BINDER LIFE STORY

One of the best ways to develop your own balance of pictures, words and life story material is using what I refer to as the ring-binder method. It consists of creating separate pages for different periods or themes in your life, and slotting them into place. A ring binder is usually the most convenient way to store this work, though you could, of course, collate it in any way that you choose. It is also a method that lends itself to compiling a life story in stages, over an extended period of time and in short or long sessions, as you choose.

Lorna, now in her eighties, has been working this way for several years, creating an account of her life. Although she is actually a professional writer, this project is definitely not for publication, but for handing down to her children and grandchildren. Her late husband's family also has a wide network of living descendents, so she has them in mind as readers too.

Lorna first of all made a chronology of her life (see p. 23). Once she had the outline, she could then work on whichever period she chose at any particular time. Each page became a visual delight, arranged with colour copies of photos and drawings from her artistic family, and written accounts and descriptions. Some entries were drawn from her journals, while others were memories that she has written up more recently for her narrative. As soon as she discovers new material to include, or thinks of another moment that she wants to record, she simply creates a new page or two and slips them into the binder in chronological order. She has now filled thirty-two ring binders using this method, something she never planned to do, but the project has grown and grown almost of its own accord. Lorna is currently working on sending each of her grandchildren a copy of the binder relating to the year in which they were born. 'They're not especially interested now,' she told me, ruefully, 'but I think they will be in years to come.'

Tip.

Keep your motivation for writing your life story at the forefront of your mind. Even if you are planning it for others, bear in mind that they may not take it up immediately, and so it's the value that you place on it which is most important at present.

3. ILLUSTRATED NARRATIVES

Most of us will want to include some photos or illustrations in a life story, but some versions can go further, so that the written narrative is largely composed around a sequence of photographs and visual material. This can still follow a chronological thread if you wish or, especially if it's of short length, may work well as a themed story, with different sections for family, special events, places you have lived and so on. In the next chapter, we will explore how to create written text to go with photographs, and it should then be clear how such an extended, heavily illustrated narrative could work. In terms of presentation, you could use a large photo album, for instance, pasting in written extracts as well as pictures, or work the other way round, using separate pages as for ordinary writing or typing, but laying them out with spaces to include the photos.

4. READY-MADE LIFE STORY BOOKS OR SCRAPBOOKS

There are many ready-produced formats that you can use to create your life story, in particular templates, which you can find via the Internet and books, rather like photo albums which are specifically designed for memoirs. These can also be found for sale online, or in some specialist craft retailers. Many originate in the USA, where recording life stories is popular.

Before you opt for one of these, do be sure to think through your life story project, and decide roughly how long you want it to be, how many photos or illustrations you would like to include and so on. It's important to match this with the specifications of the book or template. Although it can be wonderful having a ready-made mould to pour your story into, it could also restrict your output.

If you are searching for either products or templates on the Internet, try associated words in combination with the keywords 'book', 'album' and/or 'template'; suggestions are 'memory', 'life story', 'autobiography', 'memoir' and 'reminiscence'. It is also worth looking at sites which sell family-history products, and visiting family-history fairs to see the kinds of albums on offer.

5. COLLATIONS OF DIFFERENT FORMS OF NARRATIVE

You could compile a life story using existing material, such as letters or diaries, and simply create written links, explanations and an introductory section to go with them. This may be an obvious way to go if you have accumulated especially interesting letters or journals relating to a vital period of history. One woman who I taught had lived through a particularly exciting time in Burma, and she had a collection of letters sent to and from her husband, which she decided to use as the basis for her story. This might be considered more of a memoir than a life story, but it is closely related, and could be extended chronologically to include earlier and later details of your life.

Diaries and journals can also provide core material for a life story if they chronicle, for instance, a crucial time in your life. However, in my experience, journals can be tricky to work with, and may best be used to provide brief extracts within a regular written life story narrative. Most diaries are not written to be read by other people, so you will need to take out anything too personal or embarrassing (which often proves to be the case over the passage of time!). You may also need to write explanations for obscure references and edit the content for narrative flow. Diaries can be pure gold in terms of a resource, but they are not often the ideal main content for a life story. In addition, the life story is a chance to reflect on the past from the perspective of the present, and simply reproducing diary entries does not give you the same illuminating experience.

Non-written life story presentations

Although the focus of this book is chiefly on writing your life story, there are other ways that you can leave a 'footprint' of your life. Here are three popular methods:

1. A voice recording, telling your story. This can easily be made on a personal voice recorder or dictaphone, as well as on more sophisticated equipment. It can also be transcribed to produce a written account, but bear in mind that one hour of speech takes an average of six hours to type up.
2. A video recording – similar to a voice recording in terms of telling your story, this has the added advantage of actually showing you, as well as any images of other items you wish to include, such as maps, photos, places, etc.
3. A memory box, in which you place items such as personal possessions, photos and documents which have significance. You may also need to include notes on them, and to say what

each represents. The memory box is a good choice if you or the person you are helping has a limited time in which to work due to illness, and it is also much less demanding on energy and stamina. Memory-box projects are already well under way in parts of Africa, with the help of charities such as the Red Cross, where AIDS threatens the life of parents of young children, and cultural and family histories are being lost. Mothers who are diagnosed with AIDS are encouraged to create a treasure chest of family photographs, letters, stories and history.

Getting Professional Help

If you think you might want help with writing or recording your life story, above and beyond what this book can offer you, there are professional services available. For written life stories, this can simply be a case of mentoring and guidance, but you can also employ a skilled writer to do the job for you. See Resources (pp. 191, 196) for details of my life story consultancy and those of other companies offering these facilities. Some of these will also produce and print your life story for you.

Both voice and video recordings can also be made by professional companies, and they may offer the choice of recording interviews which they will transcribe and turn into a publication.

Be aware that using professional services will not be a cheap option, as you will be signing up for many hours of work done on your behalf at a professional rate. All reputable companies, however, will give you a costing in advance and, in many cases, will give you options for expanding or limiting their service, so that you know where you stand and can tailor the job to your budget.

Gathering Material For Your Life Story

As you begin to plan your life story, do start to collect together items that may be useful in composing it. You can scan, copy or insert them directly into your narrative, or just use them to refer to in your writing.

Another option is to make a selection of these and save them in a box or file which will be kept alongside your narrative.

Examples of useful items include:

- photographs
- postcards
- letters written to or by you
- newspaper and magazine cuttings
- emails
- invitations (to parties, weddings, exhibitions)
- art work
- poems
- children's school and art work (also grandchildren's)
- documents (e.g. copies of birth certificates, identity cards)
- pages from journals and diaries
- tickets (travel, theatre, lottery win)
- programmes (concerts, plays, other entertainment)
- items from your travels (tickets, papers, pictures)
- maps, plans
- recipes
- brochures for venues, houses, journeys, etc. that have featured in your life.

Producing Your Life Story

Once you have finished all the hard work of completing your life story, you may want to think about how to copy or reproduce it, or even get it into print for private circulation. The main options for doing this, which will be discussed in more detail below, are:

- producing photocopied versions of your life story
- publishing your book privately through a 'print-on-demand' service
- using a ready-made template or memory book
- keeping it in electronic form, making CDs or DVDs, or posting it on the Internet.

Photocopied life stories

This is a relatively cheap and simple option. Once you have a fair copy of your life story, whether hand- or typewritten, you can take it to a copy shop, of the kind found in most town centres, where they will print off as many copies as you want. These can be collated at the time, so that you don't have the bother of putting all the pages in order. The more pages copied, the cheaper the cost of each page. Most copy centres have a list of charges that you can consult, to work out what the optimum number of copies is for you cost-wise.

You can copy black and white photos and pictures in exactly the same way, either as pages of images to insert into your narrative, or in mixed-media pages you have created combining text and photos. Colour copying, however, is usually a lot more expensive, and you may find it more economical either to keep all the colour pictures on just a few pages, or use your home printer to reproduce them.

COVERS AND BINDINGS

If you walk away from the copy shop with your story in loose-leaf form, the chances are that you will then want to shop for some attractive binders or files to present it in. The bigger stationers and arts-and-crafts shops often have a good selection of presentation folders, so it pays to look around until you find ones that are both appealing and will suit the length of your story.

However, you can also take the process a stage further at the photocopy shop. Most offer a spiral binding service, which is an inexpensive but smart way of producing your life story in what is almost book form. You will be able to select the weight of card for the cover and choose from a range of colours. A popular option is to have the cover laminated, or overlaid with a clear sheet to protect it. Unless you are happy with a blank cover, you will need to produce a design for it, which can be as simple as just a title, either printed or in calligraphy. If you have the skills, you could also design a more decorative cover to enhance the appearance of your narrative.

If your story is slim in size, then you could request a stapled book-let version of your story, though you may have to visit a printer rather than a copy shop for this. A typical booklet would be A5 size (148mm x 210mm) and, again, it shouldn't cost you a great deal. However, this will need careful work on the layout of your text, in order to get the pages accurately arranged, as it involves folding a page double the size (A4) to create two A5 ones on each side. If you look at a pamphlet of this type (for example an order of service for a wedding), you will see how it works in practice; the first and last pages will need to be printed on the same sheet.

Finally, you might also consider having your photocopied story professionally bound by a printer, in the way that academic disserta-tions are produced. Local printers often offer this service, and there are plenty of firms offering it through the Internet as well, either in hard or soft covers. Colours tend to be sober, and bindings in library style, but the result can be dignified and impressive. The cost is relatively high, but you will have a durable volume (or volumes) to hand out to friends and family.

Print-on-demand technology

If you would like to print a number of copies of your work in book form, then you might like to consider using the recently developed technology known as 'print-on-demand'. This produces books which look like those you might find on any bookshop shelf, and the print run can be for as few or as many copies as you like. You can also re-order copies almost instantly, hence the expression 'print-on-demand'. It is likely to cost you a minimum of several hundred pounds to go down this route, but the end results are excellent, and if you plan to order anything upwards of fifty copies, the cost per copy is likely to be reasonable. Further details, including those of some suitable publish-ers, are listed in the Resources section.

The only major drawback is that, at present, standard print-on-demand books usually include colour only on the cover, though putting in black and white illustrations on the text pages is no problem.

But the technology is improving all the time, and some internet based companies now offer easy templates which you can use to create your own life story book, including colour images. You can then order printed copies on line.

CDs, DVDs and the Internet

Burning your life story on to a CD or DVD is a very convenient way to copy or distribute your life story, and you may even find that they act as bait to tempt the younger, more electronically minded members of your family to look at it! You might simply save a word-processed version of your story this way, or you could scan a heavily illustrated ring binder life story on to the computer and thence on to a disc. (If your project is a ring-binder one, it is worth considering paying to have it professionally scanned if you cannot do it yourself, as it is a good way to preserve back-up copies.)

If you are a computer graphics whizz, you may be able to devise an exciting life story format, bringing in animation, sound effects and voice recordings to copy on to a CD or DVD. Or, once again, you could approach a professional company to do this for you.

Finally, you can upload your story on to the Internet via a family website, a blog or by creating your own website specifically for this purpose.

As time goes on, the possibilities for electronic and Internet versions of life stories will increase, so if this is a method that interests you, keep an eye out for the latest developments.

CHAPTER THREE

Memories, Truth and Stories

Memories are the chief ingredient of your life story, so the process of recalling and putting them into words is an essential part of setting out your narrative. This may sound obvious, but it throws up some questions. Once you begin to open up the treasure chest of the past, you are faced with some puzzles as well as the golden gleam of your hoarded memories. Are memories always reliable and truthful? Do they change over the years? How do you recapture more elusive memories? And how do you describe them as faithfully as possible? These are all questions that will be tackled in this chapter, along with exercises to help you to recover memories and to give them order and context, so that you can readily incorporate them into your life story.

Once you start to ponder the past, your memories can stir up strong emotions, and they can also be bewildering in their profusion. Allow yourself time, if you can, for them to arise and for you to reflect on them. Writing a life story is a journey, and travelling the path is an important part of it; it's something that needs personal and emotional engagement, as well as the use of your rational faculties. To bring out the contours and shaping of your story you will need to open up the different chambers of your mind, and allow memories and impressions to surface freely.

Prompts

This is a term that is used to refer to triggers which can prod your memory, and help you to recover both complete memories and also aspects of them which you thought you'd forgotten. Broadly speaking, prompts fall into four categories:

- **Questions** These are often literal, and may relate directly to your past. 'Do you remember when we got caught smoking in the boiler shed?' an old schoolfriend asks. You'd quite forgotten, as it happens, but now it all comes back.
- **Objects** These can be anything from a wedding ring, a childhood toy, a tree in the road where you once lived, or a box of old theatre programmes. They all carry memories, and may encapsulate a certain phase of your life. Contact with them can evoke those memories.
- **Activities** These could be rowing on the river, having not held a pair of oars in your hands for thirty years; cooking a recipe that your mother showed you when you were first old enough to use the oven; or having to lift bales of hay again in the way you used to when you worked on a farm as a student.
- **Experiences** These are associated with the past and often intensely bound up with the senses, especially taste and smell, so that the scent of a lily, or the taste of freshly caught trout transports you back to another time and place. Seeing and touching are also important: it could be a view that you haven't seen for many years which reminds you of a visit to the same hilltop long ago, or the feel of a rough blanket under your fingers which suddenly brings back the narrow iron bed that you used to sleep in at your grandmother's.

MEMORY TOOLS

Keep a notebook with you whenever possible. Memories are elusive – they come and go, so don't let them slip away again without recording them. You can also use a voice recorder (sometimes found on a mobile phone, for instance) or dictaphone. These are ideal for capturing a few thoughts or recollections.

Working with prompts

Even though there is some overlap between the categories outlined above, i.e. questions, objects, activities and experiences, defining them separately gives you a framework – a system of prompts – which you can actively use to retrieve memories. This leads on to a further distinction, whereby prompts can either occur spontaneously, in the natural course of life, or they can be set up deliberately. Let's compare the two.

Here's an example of a spontaneous prompt: you turn on the radio and hear an old song that was popular when you broke up with your first girl- or boyfriend. You haven't heard it since, and it stirs up a tide of memories for you. In fact, you now recall that it was playing at the party when you were given the push. It brings back the atmosphere of that night, the sight of everyone else dancing happily, and the needle-sharp emotions that assailed you. It might even throw up details of what you were wearing, and the weather outside as you walked home afterwards, alone.

Now, here is a deliberate prompt: you decide to listen to some music, perhaps several pieces that have meant a lot to you at different times in your life. You've given it some thought, made your shortlist, tracked down recordings and have them ready at hand. The phone is switched off, no interruptions are expected, and for an hour or two, you will yield to the forces of memory and discover what this music can bring back to mind. As it begins to work its magic, you have a notepad at the ready so you can jot down any images or details associated with it. This may be a fickle process, and some melodies may not touch you at all this time round, whereas others may be almost overwhelming.

Here are a number of ways in which to jog your memory; you'll note that they can stimulate different senses, including taste and smell. You will be able to think of others, and I'll also be expanding on some of the ideas listed below.

- Revisit places where you have lived, worked or studied.
- Attend reunions or gatherings of relatives or old friends.
- Draw a map, from memory, of the neighbourhood you lived in as a child.
- Draw floor plans, from memory, of any houses you have lived in.
- Open up boxes, trunks and drawers to search out old objects you may have forgotten about.
- Chat to brothers and sisters about your shared past.
- Play music that has held meaning for you.
- Reread a few old story books from childhood.
- Try eating foods from your early years – e.g. macaroni cheese, junket, bread and dripping.
- Look at vintage household items, packaging, clothing, etc. in bric-a-brac shops, museums and flea markets.
- Take notice of any evocative scent which comes your way, when you're out for a walk or cooking, for instance. Allow it to call up associations from the past.

When using prompts, or responding to them, don't push too much. It's a subtle art, and you may find that trying too hard cuts off the flow of memory. Rather like finding a misplaced object around the house, it may work better if you turn your attention elsewhere for a few minutes and, hey presto, the wanted recollection surfaces. You know suddenly where you put the scissors – or in this case, you can now put a name to the face in the photograph.

Another common phenomenon is that memory does not always

surface immediately and completely. I often find that a memory takes time to emerge from the shadows. First I get a vague sense of it, then a few fragments float up, and then finally – if I'm lucky – it materialises in a form which is clear and whole enough to recognise or use. The process can take days, so be patient if you can't recapture it all at first.

REVISITING THE PAST

Writing your life story gives you a great excuse to visit old haunts. The town where I spent the first eight years of my life holds a very special meaning for me, and I have been back to it at intervals during my adult years. Sandwich, one of the old Cinque Ports on the Kent coast, was an idyllic childhood environment, and I often played on the street (much safer then, and far fewer cars), explored its little alleyways and quaintly named streets and generally had the run of the town. Although I have revisited it a number of times, it never fails to work its magic when I return. The smell of the river mud, the fish-and-chip shop on the corner, the railings we tied our skipping ropes to, the sound of the church bells – I could go on and on. Smells, sights and sounds all bring back memories for me, some vivid, others more elusive and misty.

If you have the opportunity to visit places where you lived either as a child, or in earlier adult life, it is a wonderful chance to recapture impressions from those days. You may even be allowed to look around the house where you lived, if you are more fortunate than I was – in Sandwich, an ageing Russian prince (as I was later told) opened the door and told me that it wasn't convenient, and made it clear that it never would be!

Allow plenty of time for simply mooching around, walking the old paths and perhaps taking trips to places nearby that also formed part of your map at the time. You might actually wish to draw a few sketch maps, to link the places or streets that you knew, or the layout of a house that you manage to view. Breaks for leisurely cups of coffee can also be productive, when you can jot down your impressions while they are still fresh in your mind.

REUNIONS

Events like school, college or work reunions can acquire an extra dimension in the context of writing your life story. You can use them to try and recall further details about your old classmates once you're in their presence, or ask them to talk about their own memories, which might, in turn, bring back other recollections for you.

They can be somewhat nerve-wracking events, as you scan the faces anxiously, trying to match them to the people you recall, but they can also be inspiring and heart-warming, and may give you fresh anecdotes for your project.

In the last chapter, I mentioned a reunion that I recently attended, at a school which I went to at the age of three and left at the age of seven, so it really was in the deep past. When I returned, I was keen to write down my impressions:

> Here I meet in quick succession a dazzling array of blasts from the past, each arousing brightly coloured memories, snippets of recall, waving like flags in the breeze. Marian, who I often played with on Saturdays, and whose mother sang opera lustily as she cleaned the house. Jeffrey, whose father ran the local tobacconist's shop, which also, inexplicably, sold tennis rackets. Sometimes the memories are best kept to myself, so I refrain from telling a solid pillar of the community that I remember his big feet with flapping sandals, and a well-groomed woman how she once weed in the middle of the classroom floor.

And visual memories began to surface too:

> We had different pictures of fruit for our coat pegs, so we could identify them before we learnt to read. We drew pictures for Bible Study – I had trouble with the table legs splaying out sideways for 'The Feast of Cana', but I liked the idea of turning water into wine. We learnt simple French, using picture cards for each object. I remember the deep purple of the plum, and the soft velvet of the cushion, painted on varnished and slightly yellowed card.

If you go to a reunion, work the room; talk to as many people as you can with whom you were connected. The occasion passes quickly, so there is no time for shyness. Be ready to share memories, and even to ask how the other person remembers you at that point in your life. Getting an outsider's view can be a revelation, although it can mean some readjustment to your personal image.

YOUR EARLIEST MEMORY

People often ask, 'Where shall I begin my life story?' Your first access-ible memory can be a good place to start, so this exercise could give you a useful lead into your life story narrative. It makes use of key ques-tions as prompts.

Choose the earliest memory that you can recall. If you don't know which one that is, or for any reason would prefer not to work with it, then select one from your early years. It doesn't matter if it's a frag-ment, or if it doesn't seem to 'tell a story'. But do ask yourself the following questions:

1. How old was I?
2. Where was I at the time?
3. What was I wearing?
4. What was the room or the surroundings like?
5. What was the weather like?
6. How did I feel?

These are direct, seemingly simple questions, but they will help you to reconnect to that time, and to discover detail in the memory that you may have overlooked. You may not be able to answer them all, but con-sider each one in turn; give it weight, and see if you can respond to it. The final question is there to ensure that you don't leave yourself out of the equation. A life story needs to contain the inner experience of its subject, not just external facts.

Next, write down your memory. Describe the scene or event, and include details that have arisen from these questions. Your account will probably run for one or two paragraphs, no more. Keep to what is real for you in your memory; resist filling in from what you may have been told since. Just put in as much extra context as you need to, to make sense of it.

Cecile, a Frenchwoman by birth, did this exercise, using it to describe herself as a very young child in Vietnam, digging happily on a beach that was fringed with coconut trees. She had to mention Vietnam in order to explain why she was in a place with coconut trees and not on her native French soil. But she didn't need to say what her family was doing out there, or to quote other experiences from her time in the country. She could, of course, include any or all of that in her complete life story, but for the purposes of this exercise, the account should stay as close as possible to the bare, essential experience.

Among early memories that students have described certain themes emerge, although it's impossible to classify definitively what they are likely to consist of. Accidents, getting into trouble with one's parents, encounters with forbidding relatives, moments of triumph over one's siblings, and moments too of pure joy in life all come up frequently. Here is one such simple moment of delight: 'Sitting in a pale-blue high chair waiting for breakfast to come in. I knew it would be a boiled egg, and I was banging my spoon on the wooden tray with excitement. I felt happy.'

Surprisingly, Sarah reckons that she was between fifteen and eighteen months old at the time, and that she 'could speak a little'. Although some people are sceptical that we can retain such early memories, there seem to be many of us who do have one or two incidents that we recall from a very young age, even from babyhood. Why not? The ability to retain 'continuous' memory, from which we can recall the complete thread of our story, may well not come into play until seven or eight years old, but we are likely to have some memories at least from earlier childhood.

Colin remembers trouble and triumph in equal measure:

One of my earliest memories is when I was aged about four or five, and on a holiday at St Anne's, on the Lancashire coast. I was with my parents and my sister Elizabeth, two years older. We were at a sizeable paddling pool along the promenade.

Elizabeth, as older sisters are likely to do, said, 'I bet I can beat you to the far end of the paddling pool!' I thought that the best way of winning was to get out at the shallow end and run around to the far end, which is what I did, not realising that the water got progressively deeper, with the result that when I jumped in the water came up to my waist. I emerged with my clothes sopping wet and got into trouble for that – but I had won!

You may find that revisiting this early memory jogs another one, and another. It can be both exciting and irritating as you concentrate on one episode, to have two or three more come up in your mind that you can't give attention to just yet. If you are afraid that you may forget these other memories, simply jot down a few words or make a voice memo to act as prompts later, when you're ready to explore and perhaps write them down in full.

The Senses and Memory

Memories are often bound up with the senses, as mentioned earlier, and you can use those sensory triggers to get back inside the experiences of your past. Smell is particularly important, and scientists recognise it as an early sense in terms of human evolution, and the one most closely allied to memory. It can help to shape basic relationships too, playing a part in mother and baby bonding, for instance, and in sexual attraction and repulsion.

Both the smell and taste of melon catapult me instantly back to the time when I was seven years old. It is bound up with a very unhappy evening spent in a hotel owned by the father of a school friend. It was a great treat to be staying in this seaside palace of luxury – or so I thought at the time, though in reality it was full of threadbare carpets and populated with elderly guests – and I was thrilled when supper was brought to me in bed on a tray, having chosen from the menu just like a grown-up. The meal began with a slice of melon, from which I spooned juicy mouthfuls, feeling very sophisticated.

Then two boys burst into the room, a pair of bullying brothers a few years older than me, who were also staying at the hotel. My friend was away somewhere for the night, so I couldn't look to her for help. They were full of themselves, having just been to see a film about the bloody battles of King Arthur and his knights, and were in the mood to terrorise a gullible little girl.

'We're going to come in during the night when you're asleep and stab you to death,' they said. 'Just like they did in the film.' I didn't know whether to believe them or not, but the effect was exactly as they'd planned – I was terrified. Now, whenever melon is in front of me again, despite the countless times I've eaten it since, its scent and taste catches me and brings back the memory of that night.

Even unhappy memories can have a kind of potency that people are drawn to explore. But many are happy; here is how one student, Belinda, associates the scent of sweet peas:

> The smell of sweet peas always takes me back to the happy summer holidays when we lived at Penhill, north Devon, where my father had a market garden. Sweet peas were one of the crops he grew to sell commercially, and I have lovely memories of helping to pick and bunch them with my mother and sister. Penhill was a beautiful and happy place. I loved the garden with my mother's herbaceous border, the rose beds, shrubbery, fuchsia hedge, rockery, and huge walled kitchen garden with its asparagus bed and raspberry canes. I would have been approximately eleven years old, and I think of sweet peas as being quintessentially English.

Belinda's narrative transports us too into the serene, flower-filled paradise of an English market garden in summer; we want to smell the sweet peas and pick the ripe raspberries. If you write directly from your own sensory memories, and allow the immediate associations to round out your description as she does, you invite the reader to join you in the experience you are describing. There is no need to strive for something very literary or clever: by communicating the essence of your own experience, you create a vivid world that another person can also step into.

Exercise: taste or smell

Choose a taste or a smell which has strong associations for you. It should be from an earlier time in your life, but not necessarily child-hood. It can be pleasant or unpleasant, and can relate to just one experience (of which the melon was an example) or something that was significant to you over a period of time (as with the sweet peas). Take a few minutes to conjure up the taste or smell in your mind, or, if you are able to have the real thing to hand (a slice of melon, a bunch of sweet peas), so much the better. Recall the experiences connected with it; make a few notes if you need to. Then write anything from three sentences to a full paragraph about it.

COLOUR

If you would like to extend the exercise, try entering the world of colour, of memories that are especially linked to colour. Here are two ways that you can approach them:

A colour event This is an occasion in which colour played a leading role, and where you remember the colour itself clearly. Janet, for instance, recalls how her mother refused to buy her a beautiful pink party dress that she longed for, and insisted on choosing a dull blue and white striped one instead. Sarah remembers a hot day in childhood, when she sat on a river bank admiring her new red shoes, and the cool waters flowing below. She thought the experience would be even nicer if she dipped her shoes in the water. Her mother didn't agree, and her bliss was shattered as she was hauled out with a scolding. Pink dress and red shoes have remained etched indelibly in the minds of these two ladies; the pink and the red colours are still vivid to them.

Using the same exercise as you did for taste and smell (above), bring back the memory using colour – ask yourself the simple, rele-vant questions listed on p. 45, and write a few sentences or a paragraph on the event.

A colour in your life Choose a particular colour and think about the associations it has had for you in your life. It could be general, for example, 'green', or more specific, for example, 'pale blue'. Try to connect with the energy of that colour and let it draw you into its own world. As memories and connections start to arise, note them down. When you have anything from three to seven associations, you are ready to start the exercise. Write it as a form of reminiscence: 'Yellow for me speaks of the huge sunflowers that my grandfather grew on his allotment. It's also a colour that my mother said I couldn't wear when I was a teenager, because it made my skin look muddy – I was upset as I really fancied a bright yellow shift dress. It was also the colour my husband and I chose to paint the nursery when I was expecting our first child. We wanted it to be a happy and sunny room for our baby.' Although these free-ranging colour memories may not be quite as intense as those to do with smell and taste, they can, nevertheless, trigger emotions and details of recall that had previously been well below the surface, so be prepared for a few tears or nostalgic moments. As with the previous exercise, a paragraph is enough; any more and you will be tempted to turn it into something else, diluting the immediacy of your descriptions. Stay with the vividness of the memories themselves.

Memories – Truth or Fiction?

Can you be certain that all your memories are true, in the literal, factual sense? Have you perhaps embroidered and edited them? Might you be 'remembering' things that you were told about, but of which you have no first-hand memories at all? My father could remember sheltering from bombs in the family cellar during the First World War, but as he was less than two years old at the time, he thought that it was his mother's oft-repeated account of the event which had gradually become his own 'memory'. He was, in any case, resistant to the idea that we retain very early memories, though arguably it was his own genuine memory.

It is an uncomfortable fact though that we all do alter the malleable substance of memory, squeezing its clay into different shapes and perhaps decorating it in different colours from its original ones. Six people in the UK who had kept diaries during the Second World

War for the 'Mass Observation' project (an archive of the lives and experiences of ordinary people) were asked, thirty years later, to recount certain episodes again without looking at any of their original notes. The researchers concluded, rather sadly, that any similarities between the old and new accounts were 'entirely coincidental', and that people had unwittingly dramatised their memories, tending to move themselves closer to the centre of the action. So, for example, bombs which had fallen in the next street were now remembered as exploding in the street where the diarist lived, or even as scoring a direct hit on the family home.

This is something we all do, usually in all innocence and with no intent to deceive. A scriptwriter for the long-running BBC radio soap, 'The Archers', told me that she believes its success is due to 'the immense human appetite for stories'. When we recount our memories, either to ourselves or to others, we make stories out of them. Sometimes we even fill in complete gaps in memory with a fabrication, a process known in psychology as 'confabulation'.

It's inevitable that our memories will not be a full and literal account of our lives, and we have to write life stories knowing this, and being aware that recall may have shifted over the years. We can make an honest attempt to recapture original details, and the exercises suggested in this chapter will certainly help with that, but the account will never be one hundred per cent accurate. However, you are writing from *your* memory and experience, not recording a documentary film, so if your life story rings true to you, it is genuine, and will, therefore, almost certainly be of interest to others in the way that an impersonal, purely factual account can never be.

Family myths and memories

Getting your family in on the act can also add to the complexity. Family stories grow up around events, and it's not surprising that parents, siblings and even children can all have divergent memories of what happened. A woman in my class, for instance, recounted a tale about her two brothers who, as young lads, saved a swimmer from drowning in a rocky bay: each brother now claims to have been the one who rescued the swimmer from the water, while the other ran for help. And, just recently, I had a lively debate with my two children, now in their thirties, as to what exactly happened in my son's troubled final term at school, when he was sixteen. He remembers a few harmless schoolboy pranks, whereas I recall one awful misdemeanour after another, of near-criminal proportions, and grim meetings with the head teacher who finally expelled him. My daughter remembers episodes in the saga that we had both forgotten. She only remembers the funny parts, I have over-dramatised it, and my son has played it down; between us we have a fuller account, but it's doubtful if we could ever recapture the whole story.

It can be a minefield, talking to other members of your family in order to recapture your past before you write it down, and my advice would be: don't attempt it. By all means check names, dates and places, and do chat to your relatives in an easy and general way about the past, but not to have them 'confirm' your story. If you want to write your life story, accept that it is just that – *your* story – and that it is not helpful (or even necessarily truthful) to impose someone else's version on top of it. Aim, as far as possible, for your core memories, your essential view, which will be truthful in its own way.

Conflicting sources of memory

Reunions, mentioned earlier, are another source for comparing and filling out old memories. Be prepared here too for varying accounts of events, even though there is unlikely to be the same degree of emotional conflict as when a family pieces together its recollections. Reflecting on my school reunion, I found it fascinating to see how personal memory interacts with that of the group:

Memory is a trickster, artful in layering recollections together. As the former pupils dig into the detail over the next two days, we find gaps and clashes in our narratives as well as concurrences. Some things we all remember – Swedish drill in the playground, the new classroom being built and the bad temper of Miss Cowell, the headmistress. One person remembers elocution lessons, and the rest of us deny that we ever had them. With difficulty, we recall that the art teacher was called Miss Painter (yes, really). Only I seem to recall the big drawstring bag, holding masses of polished wooden bricks, some shaped like arches and pillars, with which you could build impressive structures. (Must check the contact list to see if anyone became an architect.) But I wasn't alone in recalling 'Music and Movement', broadcast through primitive speakers. 'The sun is out, children, so skip, skip! Oh dear – now a rain cloud is coming! Jump over the puddles.'

Ultimately, it is up to you whether you keep strictly to your own account of events in your narrative, or whether you will round it out with the memories of others. There is no right or wrong here; it's important to be as truthful as you can, if you want your life story to be a genuine account, but since it can never be the whole, literal truth, there is scope for selecting whatever you feel to be most relevant.

Exercise: remembering backwards

The ability of memory to leapfrog from one event to another is one that you can train if you wish to gain greater recall of the past. This exercise should be practised just before you go to sleep at night. It may seem a strange time to do it, but it's when you hover on the edge of consciousness, and when deeper memories may be accessible to you as you release the clutter of everyday thoughts. It's an exercise that can have fascinating results, in terms of recovering memories and revisiting past experience. But be prepared for a yawn or two along the way, as it can also be very boring in the early stages!

FIRST STAGE
It's essential to work patiently on the preliminary stages of the exercise in order to benefit from it. Once you have turned off the light and are

settling down for sleep, cast your mind back over the last hour or so before you went to bed. Work *backwards* through this, so that you remember, for instance, brushing your teeth in the bathroom just now, and before that going upstairs, and prior to that giving the cat a dish of munchies. You won't actually be *seeing* it all in reverse, watching the toothpaste go back into the tube, but you will replay one activity preceded by another, each micro-phase witnessed again in your memory followed by the one before it. And it's necessary to go there, really to go there in your memory. It's not enough just to take yourself through a mental checklist – 'Oh yes, before that I would have stacked up the newspapers, and I probably switched off the TV standby'; you must genuinely re-engage with each memory and watch it unfold in your mind. As I said, it really is very boring, unless you have a particularly exciting way of life in the late evening.

You will probably find that you fall asleep before you've got very far, and this is fine. The soporific effect is a bonus of this exercise! And the process will continue working as you sleep, creating access to deeper levels of memory and opening gateways to the past. You may find even in the early stages that you have interesting dreams, and it's worth noting these down.

LATER PRACTICE

Once you have practised this exercise for a month or so, preferably every night, you are ready to move on to the next stage. If you can already remember backwards through a whole day, you are doing really well. From there, you can move back to the day before, and the one before that, and so on. But you are ready now to progress to leapfrogging, going back through the chain of memory associations, and seeing where they lead you.

As you work your way patiently backwards through the recent hours, be on the alert for any other memories triggered from further back in time. When one arises, drop the recent sequence and jump back to the associated memory that has come to mind. For instance, if I'm recalling washing up the tea cups last thing at night, a memory of washing up a sink full of crockery during my first holiday job at a golf club may suddenly appear. I then replay as much about that as I can.

Most probably another memory will be stirred by that one; I remember, for instance, that the golf club was in a huge, semi-wild park, where I was often sent to walk the family dog. I remember exploring a wood there, and my favourite oak tree in it. Then an image comes up of riding in that park, and being out with a group from the riding school when a classmate of mine fell off her pony and broke her collarbone. Perhaps the memory then shifts to an earlier time, before I learnt to ride, but created a stable full of imaginary horses with a playmate.

The important thing is to catch each memory as an entity, whether it's a specific event or a phase of your life and to go there, revisiting the experience and replaying it in your mind. See as much of it as you can visually; engage the senses. Don't let it speed up too much, even though you may be tempted to race back through it and follow where it leads you. The trail can become very exciting, but you need to connect with the substance of each memory for the process to be effective.

If you encounter a very difficult or painful memory, do what you can in terms of re-entering it, but do so with a neutral overview. You may be reliving the memory to some extent, but it *is* in the past, and the observer in you can simply watch it dispassionately at one level, even though there may be strong feelings embedded in it. And don't be tempted to analyse the memories while you're in the middle of the exercise, or you will lose the immediacy and it will become less effective. Trust the process to work in its own way, to liberate old memories from any earlier edits you may have made, or to throw off old judgements that you attached to them.

Once again, the 'leapfrogging' should tail off quite naturally into sleep, but if it doesn't, you can gently let the exercise go at any point.

Here are some of the effects and benefits of remembering backwards:

- It can throw up earlier memories that you had forgotten.
- It can round out old memories.
- You may have interesting or vivid dreams.
- You may get to sleep more easily.

- It is a good exercise for the mind and memory in general.
- It can dissolve old thought patterns or viewpoints that blocked you from seeing the bigger picture.

Working with Photographs

Earlier in the chapter, we looked at the theme of working with prompts, and now we can use this in the context of photographs. This section will help you to get 'inside' a photograph again, and also to create a narrative for it that you can use in your life story if you wish.

Most life stories will include some photographs; sometimes people prefer to construct their whole story around them, with text simply to link them, allowing the images themselves to tell the tale. Whichever form your life story takes, photographs will be much appreciated by your readers, and can easily be included in photocopies or even in a printed edition of your story (see Chapter Two, pp. 37–38, and Resources, pp. 198–199).

Before you embark on choosing the whole range of photos to put into your story, I suggest that you begin by taking between five and ten photos pictures from your collection. Choose at least two that you feature in, and at least one of your family in your childhood, if possible. You could also select one of your current family set-up. Each of the photographs needs to be significant to *you*. Don't choose them out of duty, or simply to spin a good yarn. Make sure each picture has meaning, even if it's only a blurred picture of two little children on the beach. That was you and your brother, taken on the first day you managed to lift your feet off the bottom and swim a yard or two, and you remember only too well how you caught a wriggly starfish and then the sand got in your sandwiches afterwards . . . You recall the day with pride and affection, and there is an added poignancy since, soon afterwards, your family moved house and you never again saw that idyllic beach of which you have many other happy memories.

There – the work is practically done already! This is the kind of narrative that you can write up around a photograph. But before you get started, consider the following questions; they are similar to those that we used earlier in writing about an early memory, and they will help to construct the bones of the narrative, so don't be tempted to skip them.

- Who is in the photo?
- When was it taken?
- What are you/the people doing in it?
- What does it mean to you?

The last question is particularly important, as it's the reason why you're including the photo.

Test this out with one photo of your choice, and write anything from three or four sentences to a full paragraph – no more, otherwise the text will outweigh the image, whereas it should enhance it like a picture frame.

You are writing this ultimately for your readers, so once you have completed the description for your photo, check it out with a more objective eye, and see if there is anything that they might want to know, or will naturally ask about it. 'Why were you in Birmingham that day when you lived in Stockport?' 'Who is that strange character on the right in the picture?' 'Did your father always wear funny hats?' and so on. You don't have to reveal everything, but you do need to set the context.

Now, or at a later stage, you can add a key to the people in the photograph, with names in order, or write a caption to head up the narrative. But do this after you've written the first description, which comes from your direct connection to the photograph. Otherwise, you could dull the intensity of your response.

Next, continue with your other photos, until you've completed a small assortment. This core collection will act as a model for describing further pictures for your narrative when you're ready to tackle the whole story. If you do too many at once, you may lose some of the careful attention and loving care that you put into these first few pictures – they are your touchstone, and when you go back to the project, they'll remind you of how you want to choose and write up additional images.

Examples of working with photographs

Jennifer showed us two photos, which between them tell a story. Here is what she wrote:

> *Photo One*: this is a photo of my twin brother Jack and me. We are about four to five years old, and we are in the garden of our house in Bushey. Jack seems to be propping up the archway that went over a path. As we grew older, we did very little together, as he was a very keen sportsman and went to a boys' prep school, where he became dedicated to cricket. We always quarrelled a lot, and I would try to win the argument by saying, 'I am five minutes older than you,' which was what my mother had told me.

> *Photo Two*: this is a picture of Jack, probably taken when he was captain of cricket at his school. I suppose he was about sixteen years old. This makes me feel sad, as he was killed in a motor-cycle accident in the army in 1943, aged twenty.

Some photos can be extraordinary documents in their own right – a combination of personal history and world events. Fenella, who served in the RAF for thirty-three years, has a picture of herself with her fellow officers, all eating their picnic lunch around a swimming pool. There is a palm tree in the foreground, and a large colonnaded building behind. She showed it to the rest of the class, and at first sight, it seemed nothing remarkable – perhaps they were on duty abroad, having a meal break at a local hotel. Then Fenella revealed that it was taken on 4 June 2003, and at Saddam Hussein's palace in Iraq. She was a member of the first vanguard troops sent to check out the palace, following the allied invasion of Iraq. Hussein and his henchmen had fled, but the job of the troops was still a dangerous one – to search the territory for weapons, or whatever else might be lurking there. Despite the apparent opulence of the pool and palace in the photo, it does look rougher on closer scrutiny, and, in fact, Fenella tells how they found the whole place smashed and looted, with only one door remaining in the entire building.

Here are my preliminary notes for a photo from my own collection, which shows the process of musing on the picture, describing it and even adding in a little research. From these notes, I can then go forward to write a more polished, integrated description if I wish.

The photo was taken at a party in our street in Cambridge to celebrate the Queen's Silver Jubilee. It was a glorious day, with all our friends and neighbours out on the street, many in fancy dress. I am in the middle, bending forward to hold my little girl by the hand, who is wearing a kind of Bo Peep costume. (I had a vintage clothing shop at the time, which came in very useful for dressing up.) At first, I couldn't remember the date, but thanks to the wonders of the Internet, was able to find it in a few seconds: 7 June 1977.

The entry also carried accounts of the day: The Queen, dressed in pink, attended a service at St Paul's, riding through the cheering crowds in her golden state coach. Although we were past the rebellious sixties, it was a time when everyone was still willing to trot out the red white and blue, and to celebrate the monarchy, even if we secretly thought it a bit quaint! Many people took the day off work, and there were street parties all over the country. At ours, we sat down to lunch at long trestle tables for which we had all supplied food and drink, and later there were children's games and races. For me, this picture symbolises a time when life seemed settled and contented, in terms of family and neighbourhood. It is also a favourite photo of my now adult children, who remember the fun of the day well, including, in my son's case, winning the egg and spoon race.

These examples of photos cover childhood and adult life, scenes both domestic and global. The scope is wide, and if you sift through your collection, you will probably find a much more interesting range of subject matter than you might expect.

KEY POINTS FOR WORKING WITH PHOTOGRAPHS

- Select just a few photos to start with.

- Pick ones that have real meaning for you.

- Choose at least one with yourself in it.

- Immerse yourself in the picture, recapture the flavour of that moment.

- Write a description of what it portrays, including some factual detail.

- Be sure to say why you have chosen it, and what it means to you.

- Be prepared for some photos to evoke strong emotions in you.

- Go back to the description, and add in other information that future readers may need to make sense of the photo.

- Add a key or a caption, if you like.

- Keep this collection of photos with their descriptions to act as a core resource for your life story, and to add to later.

Grounding the Senses

It's important not to get too lost in the past; writing your life story will mean that you spend much more time than usual contemplating earlier times and events, and it can affect your moods and even your dreams. You'll need to counterbalance this by really coming into the present again, switching your attention back fully to the world around you and the life that you live now.

So, to finish the chapter, here is an exercise that you can use before or after every session of recapturing and writing about your past. If you've followed some of the suggestions in this chapter, you'll know how crucial the senses are in this process. Likewise, they are vital in the present moment too, bringing you back fully to the here and now:

1. Take a few minutes to sit or stand at ease.
2. Breathe long and deeply, but in a relaxed fashion.
3. Pay attention to everything that your senses are telling you – open your eyes to what is around you: what sounds can you hear? What sensations do you have? What can you smell? What kind of taste do you have in your mouth?

This exercise should both ground and energise you, and, as such, is useful either before you start working (to focus you for the task ahead) or afterwards (to replenish your reserves). If you like, you can write down what you observed – a few notes or sentences which will get you in the mood for further writing at the beginning of the session, or help to root the experience if you are concluding it.

TIPS TO KEEP YOU SANE AND CHEERFUL WHILE WORKING ON YOUR LIFE STORY

- Set a time limit for your work, if you tend to go on too long, and stick to it.

- Don't brood on the past.

- Appreciate what you have now.

- At the end of each memory or writing session, use your breathing and your senses (see above) to restore energy levels and to bring you back to the present.

CHAPTER FOUR

The Blueprint Story

This is the moment when you write a short version of your life story. If you have followed the suggestions in the earlier chapters, you will by now have completed a basic chronology, written a few accounts and explored how to add text to photographs. You may also be bubbling with ideas about how to present your story. But before you start on the full-scale project, I recommend writing a blueprint story first, one that covers all major events and phases of your life. It will serve as a very useful basis for your extended narrative.

The Value of the Blueprint Story

The blueprint story that you write will be a fairly short but accurate version of your life story. This means that if, for any reason, you can't or don't wish to continue past this point, you will have a narrative that you can keep to work on later, or to pass on to family and friends just as it is. It can also become the basis for a short life story presentation; the blueprint story tends to be somewhat terse and factual, but can easily be filled out with images and a little extra text, as will be explained further on.

If you have limited time, perhaps because you are suffering from a life-threatening illness, for example, I strongly recommend that you focus your efforts first and foremost on this shorter version. It will give you peace of mind that you have completed a personal narrative, and stand as a testimony to the life you have lived.

On the other hand, if you are trying out this project now with a view to going into it more fully in later years, this is also a good reason to complete your blueprint narrative. It will be a useful and fascinating resource to take out again and work on at some future date.

The Challenges of Setting Down Your Life as Story

Before turning to the guidelines for writing a blueprint story, I'd like to take a moment to look at some of the challenges and obstacles which may arise before you even start the task, or which might rear their heads at a later stage in the writing of your life story. It's worth acquainting yourself with these common hindrances now, so that you are ready to deal with them if they do pop up along the way.

Writers' displacement activities

This one is very simple. It's the tendency of writers to find something – anything – 'urgent' to do, rather than sit down and write. If you find yourself inexplicably drawn to washing the windows instead of writing your opening paragraph, you are in good company with many famous writers. Laurie Lee, for example, was employed by the government in the Second World War to write film scripts, but his colleagues remember how he wandered up and down the corridors playing his recorder, avoiding the moment when he would have to sit down in his office and type a few words.

Getting started can be the hardest part, but you will probably thoroughly enjoy writing once you begin. So if needs be, decide on a time to begin, and stick to it. Ask yourself if it is absolutely crucial that you pay the gas bill or walk the dog first. If not, switch into writing mode and plunge in.

Accepting life as story

Although you may be interested in writing your life story, you may also be wary of accepting the idea that your life *is* a story. Why should there be this reluctance? Everyone likes stories, after all. But a story has a beginning and an end, and although the beginning is fine, nobody really wants to think of their story as having an end. Not yet, at any rate. Some people even secretly fear that they are tempting fate by writing it down in this way, thus heralding the final act.

It might also seem that you are declaring your active, creative years over, and that there is nothing left to do now except dwell on memories. There is a sad painting by the Russian artist V. M. Maximov, in which two old ladies sit side by side, knitting and dreaming in an overgrown garden. The title, 'All's in the Past', tells you where their thoughts are, and how little else is left to them.

This is not where we are planning to go with this book! Writing your life story only requires that you tell the story, or a part of the story, as you have experienced it up to now. It is not about bringing the story to an end, so although you'll want to round off the narrative, you won't be declaring your life over in the final pages. Think of the life story as a good soap opera, or a series of books, in which the hero or heroine can return to star again in another episode! It can take courage to review and tell your story, but it does not consign you to the 'has-been' category.

If you do know that your time is short, as did patients in the hospice where I volunteered, for instance, then my sympathies are with you. But I would still encourage you to take this on as a living task, not a dying one, and to let your talents, wisdom, creativity and engagement with life shine out from it.

The question of how to define your writing

'What are you working on?' people may ask you, when they know you're involved in a writing project. 'I'm writing a life story,' you will probably answer. No problem in itself, as this is the obvious way to describe what you're doing. But once the definition is made, even if it's only in your own mind, it will almost certainly have an effect on the way that you feel about your project.

All words carry associations – some positive and some potentially negative. Names are powerful, and whatever one is given to the genre will to some extent define your expectations of how you should work, and what the goal is. In the constructive sense, 'life story' is a good term to use; it's popular, widely recognised, and benefits the writer's confidence because it encourages all of us to consider our story of value, and worth setting down. But, like any other term, it can also throw up doubts, based on what it apparently demands of us: 'I don't have an interesting story to tell', 'How can I possibly recall my whole life?' or 'I'm not sure I could write a story', are frequently heard as excuses for backing out.

But would another term be better? By way of contrast, consider what would it be like to use the word 'autobiography' instead. Would this not generate a different set of anxieties? Such as: 'I'm not famous', 'I haven't got enough to say', 'I can't include enough detail', 'How can I be objective enough?' If you choose to use 'autobiography' for your project, which, of course, you are perfectly entitled to do, it might inspire you to work very hard on your writing in terms of style and polish, but it will also create high literary expectations that could prove daunting.

Don't let the name of any genre impede your work in this way. If you find your intention wavering, remind yourself of what drew you to the project in the first place. Your passion and your interest is a flame that needs to be cherished, not dowsed in the cold water of misgivings. Remember too that there is a whole range of techniques set out in this book that you can use to navigate your way through the narrative, and that your story doesn't have to be long or literary. It doesn't have to fit into a given template, but only needs to be an authentic account of your life, in whole or part. And you are the only person qualified to do the job from first hand experience!

Any terms we use are going to have their drawbacks as well as their advantages. The words we use for the 'job description' will always affect us, both for better and for worse. We do need to name the category we are writing in, as it gives focus and purpose to the project; life story is a good term for most people to use, but choose another if it isn't right for you. Whatever name you use, though, should help you to take pride in your work, and not deter you from the task.

The pain of selection

You will almost certainly face some frustration when you discover that, in practical terms, you can't set down everything of significance in your life story. It's impossible to include it all, and you may worry that you are distorting the truth by being selective, and ignoring certain events of your life. The blueprint story is a good rehearsal for coping with this, and if you can overcome any dissatisfaction in this respect as you write it, you will find it much easier when you come to your extended narrative.

Creativity seems to be a touchstone here. You can rise above 'the pain of selection' if you keep in mind that writing your life story is a creative process. It can still be *authentic*, written from the truth of your life, even if it is selective, but your life experience, distilled through the creative process and harnessed with the help of the structure and techniques suggested here, can be turned into a wonderful and genuine personal narrative.

It also helps to cultivate a little objectivity, viewing your life from the outside, as if you were going to write up someone else's story, in the way that a journalist or a biographer would. Of course, you are also going to see it from the inside – that is your unique ability. But having elements of both will help with the structure, and to condense it into manageable proportions.

Do I really want to set down my story?

Writing your life story will inevitably affect the way that you view your life and recall it. You will be examining your memories, and they may settle down into a new pattern once you have done this. It is important to recognise this from the outset, and if you do not want to 'interfere' with the past in any way, shape or form, then this project may not be for you.

But, speaking from my own experience of writing in general, I would advise not worrying too much about this or any other challenge until the work is complete. It's normal to be beset by doubts while in the middle of the task, but once you have the finished manuscript in your hand, a sense of pride and fulfilment generally takes over.

In the course of this chapter, we'll be looking at some of the real benefits to be gained from writing your life story. It can bring back to mind parts of your life that you had largely forgotten, for instance. You may also begin to see certain threads that have run through your life, patterns which you were largely unaware of up till now. And overall, writing your narrative can give you confidence in knowing that you do indeed have a story to tell.

FOCUS AND PERSPECTIVE: CLOSE-UPS AND LONG SHOTS

Every narrative has a particular focus, and a specific perspective. An easy way to understand this is in terms of a photograph or film shot. If you crouch close up to your subject – let's say a flower growing in the grass – and use a macro lens on your camera, you can get a wonderfully sharp and detailed image of it. If you stand at the other side of the field, you'll get a panoramic shot of the landscape, and perhaps only a speck of blurred colour to indicate the flower. It's the same reality, but a different viewpoint.

Good full-length narratives include both 'long shots' and 'close-ups', which allow you to alter the pace of the writing and the detail that it includes. We'll look into this more later on, but it's worth getting familiar with the concept now, and it can help to realise that the blueprint story is mostly long shot. You may be able to sneak in a few close-ups which will enhance your narrative, but mostly you will need to keep your perspective much broader because you have a lot of ground to cover in a short time. Remember that all the events, places and people which do not feature in your blueprint story are still there in the background (like the flowers in the grass), and in an extension of your narrative, you will be able to elaborate on them much more.

If you decide to make your blueprint story the basis of your final life story, you can include photos in it, writing full captions for them in the way that we explored in the previous chapter (see p. 56), and perhaps inserting some examples of 'bubble writing' (see pp. 12–19) into your narrative. These will act as close-ups and give a varied, interesting texture to your work, so that your blueprint story can become a short but complete life story in its own right.

Time for Reflection

Symbols are a way of exploring truth intuitively, and they often throw up new meanings and associations, different to those which arise directly from words. Before beginning the blueprint story, I suggest a brief session to contemplate the nature of your individual lifetime by using one particular symbol, the spiral. Working with symbols can inspire your writing in subtle ways, and time spent with them is rarely wasted.

The spiral

In working on chronology, we've mostly been thinking in a linear way, so in order to shift this mode of perception, let's take a look at how a spiral can be seen as representing a lifespan. Time is often thought of as circular in various cultures, and even in our own, there are still good examples in seeing time as the cycle of the seasons and the years, for instance.

The spiral is circular in essence, though it's a developing, growing kind of circle, a point which wasn't lost on ancient civilisations, who often depicted the spiral in their paintings and engravings as a symbol of just that, of growth and development. It's an excellent symbol to represent a human life, and here's how you might work with it in this context:

1. Draw a spiral, beginning with the centre point and allowing it to wind round and round until it is as big as you wish; it doesn't matter how big or small.
2. Contemplate the starting point as your birth. Then, very slowly, trace the spiral moving outwards, using the point of a pencil or pen as a marker, or just with a finger. As you do so, imagine that it represents your life unfolding from birth until the present day.
3. When you have reached the outermost point of the spiral, if there is space, draw another two or three turns of it extending outwards (if not, simply imagine them). Perceive this as your future. Observe any thoughts or impressions that come up.
4. Next, sit back, look at the spiral again and ask what colours you might choose for it. You can paint or shade the spiral if you wish, and keep it to hand as a symbol of your project.
5. Finally, trace the spiral the other way, travelling in the opposite direction from outer to inner. What might this movement mean?

We'll return to the spiral again later, in Chapter Seven (see p. 149).

AN IMPORTANT NOTE ON WRITING GUIDANCE AND STYLE

There are suggestions throughout this book on how to structure your work, and how to improve your style and your narrative flow. Feel free to take as much or as little from them as you wish. There could be good reasons why you are not planning to concentrate too much on style and structure. You may already be an experienced writer, or perhaps you simply want to get the story down the way it comes out. In this case, I recommend that you skim through the key points of writing technique, which are principally given here and in Chapter Six, and take from them just the main ideas that are useful to you, and only in as much detail as you need.

Setting Down Your Blueprint Story

We've covered all the preliminaries, and there is now nothing standing between you and the blueprint story that you're going to write! Here are twelve key points relating to structure and content to bear in mind when planning your story, each one accompanied by some guidelines.

Structure

1. LENGTH

Aim to write between 1500 and 5000 words in total. If you type with single spacing, this is likely to be approximately three to ten pages. If you write by hand, do a quick check by taking a sample page, counting the average number of words on a line, and multiplying it by the number of lines on the page.

It's essential to keep the length within boundaries here. This helps you to map out your life more accurately, and means that you save the detailed narrative for your main project. It's not always easy, I know – when I created my blueprint story I found I was writing far too much, and that it would have ended up at about double the limit. So I went back to the beginning, and reduced it severely until I was back on track again. Keeping to a set length might seem tedious or unnecessary, but it does have value; it helps you to focus on the essentials, and is a useful exercise in figuring out the vital components of your story.

2. START AND FINISH POINTS

Start with your birth, and end at the current time. Even if you decide to write your life story around a shorter period, this full version will mean that you've recorded the whole length of your life to date, giving you a better perspective from which you can select a time span later on. It may also change your views about what are the most important parts of your life.

Although you don't need to give your story a title at this stage (more of that later, see p. 85), I suggest that you head it with your name, and begin it quite literally from the facts of your birth. It might look like this, for example:

John Alistair Jones

I was born on 5 July 1958 in Sidmouth, Devon. My parents were Stephen and Gillian Jones, and they already had two older children, Geoffrey and Claire.

This will give you an easy lead into your blueprint narrative. In your extended life story, you may well want to take a different starting point, such as your first memory, but this is the most effective and economical way to begin a story where you are limiting the word length.

Take the story through until the present day, through all periods of your life, and describe the current phase of your life as well. You need not give all the details, just a general sense of where you are now.

3. AND 4. USE THE FIRST PERSON AND PAST TENSE

I have put two key points together here, as they work well in tandem. Write your narrative in the first person and in the past tense: 'I was born . . . I grew up . . . I joined the army in 1968' and so on.

Even in the brief blueprint story, you still need a personal approach. (Don't forget, however, to make sure your full name does appear somewhere on the narrative! You can always use it for the heading, as suggested on p. 71.) And while it can be very effective to write some passages in the present tense either for your photos or in the extended narrative, in this short blueprint you will confuse the reader and possibly yourself if you try to switch tenses around.

5. PROPORTIONS

Make allowances for writing more about certain phases of your life, since inevitably there will be more to say about some periods than others. Your blueprint version helps you to see what these are likely to be, so that you can plan for them in your main life story narrative.

As a general rule, it's common to write more about your childhood than about a corresponding time span of your adult life. One third childhood to two thirds adult life makes up a good narrative or even half and half. You may also find that you write more about recent years than about periods of adult life further in the past. This can create an elegant shape for your story, even in blueprint form, beginning with more detail about childhood and ending with a fuller account of the recent past than for the years in between.

6. CHRONOLOGY

You've already done much of the hard work for this in Chapter Two, and now you can put it to good use as a list of reference points for events, dates and places on which to base your narrative.

The headings of 'Place', 'Family & Relationships', 'Life Events' and 'Work & Study' (see p. 22) are ideal topics to include in the blueprint story. How many reference points you can include will depend on how full your chronology is, but don't feel that you have to pack them all in; after a couple of pages, you will probably have a good sense of how many you can include.

You are unlikely to have space to include everything under additional headings, such as 'World Events', but they may give you ideas for a passing mention. For instance, in my blueprint story, I managed to squeeze in a reference to the hippy era, as it was highly relevant to my student days at Cambridge. After taking A Levels, I had been working in a hotel in Torquay:

> It was 1967; I saw girls with long hair and bells round their necks, wandering barefoot along the seafront; they were the heralds of the hippy era. And when I went up to Cambridge in October, it was to a new world.

7. CONTINUITY

Even though this will only be a short narrative, try to link together all the different periods of your life. I found the 'Place' section of the chronology a useful guideline in this respect, since I've lived in a variety of different locations during my life, each of which has defined a new phase for me. By including all the places I've lived in, I was automatically incorporating all my major life phases. If 'Place' is not your main thread, then check to see if another chronology heading works better for you.

TIPS FOR WORKING ON A COMPUTER

Saving work If you work on the computer, do save this first narrative and any subsequent ones with a file name that you can easily identify. For example, you could call your first draft of this project 'Blueprint Story 1'. Calling it simply 'Life Story' could cause confusion between files you create later, especially between the blueprint version and the extended narrative. This might sound obvious, but, believe me, as a writer I know how easy it is to start out with everything clear in your mind, then find later that you have inadvertently mixed up your files, or, worse still, lost one altogether.

Save your work every ten minutes or so, even if you have an automatic save function. When you have finished one version and want to edit it, I recommend keeping your original version as it is, and saving your newer version with a different file name, e.g. 'Blueprint Story Edit 1'. As soon as you open up the file with the intention of editing it, go to 'Save As', and choose the new name for it. You can then be sure that your original file is safe. Double-save your work: keep an extra back-up copy of all your life story files, on a CD or DVD, floppy disk, or on any back-up storage device that you may have.

Cuts You may also wish to create a file called 'Cuts'. This will give you the courage to cut passages if they are too long, or off the point. By saving them in a different location, you will know that they are there should you want to restore them later. I know one writer who keeps all of his cuts, from all of his books, articles and essays – and he keeps them for ever! Sometimes he even recycles them into other work. I don't go to those lengths, but I do like to review the 'Cuts' file from time to time to see if there are any little gems that might deserve a new lease of life.

Printing Make printouts at regular intervals, both for peace of mind, and because you can sometimes spot errors more easily on a printed page than on a screen. I prefer to do a printout after every third or fourth session. To save paper and ink, use a draft print quality if you have the facility, and print on the back of used sheets.

Content

8. GIVE PRIORITY TO FACTS

In this short narrative, the facts should predominate. The main facts of your life will be the backbone of your blueprint story. You will have plenty of opportunity in your extended narrative to include fuller descriptions, reflections and accounts.

A wise friend of mine used to say, 'Events tell a tale. Look at what people do, rather than what they say.' And the same is true in the context of this exercise: pulling out the events from your life, and narrating what has actually happened can be surprisingly illuminating. For example, I am tempted to say that I long to settle in one place, and wish I had permanent roots, but by listing all the changes of location that I've made, it becomes eminently clear that every so often, I feel the urge to uproot and seek pastures new. Seeing the patterns made by the facts of your life can draw out themes in your story that you were unaware of. We'll touch on that later, when we come to evaluate your blueprint story (see p. 82).

The chronology has given you the basis of facts to put into your narrative, but in this short version you may still need to be selective. Keep the continuity of your life's development, but remove non-essential events for now. You can always put them in later, in your full life story. Conversely, you may also need to add in more facts or events now on your chronology to create continuity; it's only when you move from your chronology to your narrative that you notice where the gaps are.

9. LIMIT YOUR 'CAST LIST'

Any life can have a cast of hundreds in it – all your family, friends, colleagues and people who have been significant to you in one way or another. For your blueprint story, you will need to scale down your cast list to a very small nucleus of people. This can cause a few wails as you strike out your best friend, your lost love and your eccentric uncle. But it's unlikely that you will be able to complete the factual story of your life in such a short space unless you do. I wrote my blueprint story in 4500 words, almost up to the limit, but I still had to leave out a number of key people. It caused me moments of anguish until I

realised that I had to do this, first in order to get to the end, and sec-
ondly because the focus must remain on 'I' rather than 'he' and 'she'.
With your blueprint story, you are spinning the thread that will form
the central strand of your extended narrative, and this has to be more
about you than anyone else.

As a general rule, the main members of the cast for your blueprint story (depending on your circumstances) are:

- your parents
- your siblings
- your partner(s) and/or spouse(s)
- any relatives, friends, lovers or colleagues who are crucial to
  events (there may well be none that you need to include at this
  stage)
- your children.

You may find that you have space to include one or two more characters to improve the storyline, but start only with those listed above, and
see how you get on.

ACKNOWLEDGING THE CHARACTERS IN YOUR STORY

This exercise can help if you find it difficult or painful to
leave people out, but it is also rewarding to do in its own
right. It indicates acceptance of all the people in your
life, and a respect for the part that they have played in it:

Close your eyes, and think of some of the most
important people in your life, past and present. Call
them to mind singly first of all, and then, as the
numbers grow, see them as a group. Recognise their
significance to you, in whatever form that may have

been, and acknowledge to yourself that you will bring them into your story if you can and, if not, that they will still be in your heart.

Note: although you may be tempted only to include those whom you love in this exercise, perhaps you should not exclude some of those who have given you trouble or caused pain, since through these encounters you may have learnt valuable lessons. Perhaps this, too, can be a form of love?

10. LINKING PARAGRAPHS

By turning a list of dates into a narrative you are casting yourself in the role of storyteller. So even in this blueprint story, it's important to practise creating a narrative flow. The following guidelines on how to link paragraphs, and give continuity, may be useful in this respect; if you simply absorb the general drift now, you can refer to them either if you get stuck at a particular point, or when you reread and edit your work later.

There are four main ways to link your paragraphs together. You can:

- interweave them
- create a deliberate contrast, or a break of mood or theme between them
- continue your theme naturally from one to the next
- use connecting phrases.

Interweave your paragraphs. This method is easiest to see by example, so here are the paragraphs which precede and follow the passage that I quoted on p. 73 from my blueprint story:

I had a serious boyfriend in my last year at school, after years of crushes, short-lived romances and awkward dates. He was an ambulance driver called Bob, an 'older man' of twenty-six. We went to jazz clubs, stock-car racing and once to meet his only relative, a crazy elderly aunt in Lincolnshire, who lived with twenty cats in a dilapidated cottage.

Our relationship began to cool off when I spent the summer after A Levels working in hotels in Torquay, where I had already made friends and there was a great folk club scene. It was 1967; I saw girls with long hair and bells round their necks, wandering barefoot along the seafront; they were the heralds of the hippy era. And when I went up to Cambridge in October, it was to a new world.

Here I plunged into the alternative culture as well as into my studies. I began in conventional fashion, by writing an article for *Varsity* magazine, acting in the Mummers drama society, and even going to lectures. By the end of the second term, I had joined a street-theatre protest group, listened to 'underground' music and dressed in vintage clothes from Oxfam.

I've linked the first paragraph to the second by continuing the theme of the boyfriend. Then, in order to move smoothly into the third paragraph, I've embedded the change from the summer break to university at the end of the second one, which gives me a springboard to link these two paragraphs. And the 'hippy' theme begun in Torquay also creates a flow from one paragraph to the next. It wasn't an essential point to mention about my summer stay in Torquay, but I realised that it would give good 'lift-off' into the description of the new world I entered in Cambridge, where my experience was intensely affected by the culture of the late sixties.

Create a deliberate contrast. This can be a very effective way of giving a paragraph a crisp new start, lending more punch to the narrative. For instance, it may work well if you are talking about a change of scene, house move or an unexpected event in your life, such as a death or accident. Although, in one sense, this is a break between paragraphs, it is not total discontinuity. The paragraphs are linked by this contrast, like changing from one key to another in music, but into a key which is still part of the overall harmony of the piece. The shift of focus from one theme to the next should be just enough to create a little shock for the reader, igniting a spark that jumps like electricity from one paragraph to the next.

Allow paragraphs to flow naturally from one to the other. This works especially well if you are simply continuing the same theme. In the blueprint story, you may not have too much opportunity for this kind of continuity as you have to pack a lot into a short space, and paragraphs will often be self-contained passages on a particular topic. So enjoy the chance where you can!

Use connecting phrases. This helps to smooth the way from one paragraph to the next, and to prevent any changes from being too abrupt. Words or phrases to do with time can be useful, such as: 'By this time (I was doing such-and-such)'; 'From the age of (thirty)' or 'Two years later (we moved to xyz)'. Then words such as 'Although', 'But' and 'However' are useful in helping to bridge contrasting ideas. You might wish to look out for other examples of connecting devices in books or articles that you are reading, and make a note of any that seem useful.

11. REFLECTIONS AND COMMENTS

By now, it will have become clear that the blueprint story has to be concise and factual. But there *is* scope for weaving in a few questions and reflections, an element which you will want to include more in your extended life story, and which is a key ingredient of the very best memoirs and autobiographies. It's worth practising writing them here, even if there is only enough room for a few musings. They will need to be kept as passing comments, but you will be able to fill them out in the complete narrative later on.

To insert your take on events you can try using:

- questions
- comments
- observations
- explanations
- reflections

This list is not exhaustive, and there is some overlap; this is fine though, as they can add different layers of meaning to your narrative. Even as a very brief aside, or in embryonic form, they can work well in the blueprint story, and be vital pointers to themes that you would like to develop later.

As a simple example, I made the following observation when I was writing about the move that my first husband and I made with our children to the countryside, followed several years later by another move back to the city: ' . . . My own commitment was wavering. I learnt that I loved nature, but was not so keen on the hard slog needed to live a truly rural way of life.'

Writing this gives the explanation as to why we moved; in the narrative it would have seemed strange if I had switched from life on Exmoor to the city of Bristol without giving any reasons. It is also an observation about my own learning process. There is a lot more that I could say about this experience, but it would have to be saved for a longer narrative.

12. WRITE TO BE READ!

You may not want to show your first attempt at a life story to anyone, and you don't have to. But write it *as if* it's going to be read. Have an imaginary reader waiting, who is really keen to read your story. It will pay off – you'll develop a better eye for ensuring that your narrative is continuous and that it makes sense. You will become more aware of important details that you need to give for the sake of your readers, such as names and places that you may otherwise be tempted to skip because you are so familiar with them. What you take for granted might be a mystery to them.

You are also turning your life into story, and stories are meant, by their very nature, to be told, read and understood by other people. You are plying a craft, practising a skill, creating magic by weaving the story of your life into a tapestry that others can be intrigued and inspired by. Keeping your reader in mind should help, not hinder your writing, but there are some points to watch, to ensure that this is a constructive approach, and not one that will inhibit you:

- Don't restrict the facts you put in because it may be read by someone else (e.g. because you think an event or experience might be too trivial), unless the memories are really private or confidential.
- Imagine your reader as kindly, interested and benign, not as judgemental or disapproving.
- Keep your style as natural as possible. Don't try to make it artificially literary or journalistic, just because it may have a readership.
- Put your work away at intervals, or when you finish a section, and come back to it later with a fresh eye. This will help you to see it more objectively.

AT A GLANCE – KEY POINTS FOR YOUR BLUEPRINT STORY

STRUCTURE

- Keep the length to between 1500 and 5000 words.

- Start with your birth and end at the current time.

- Use the first person, 'I'.

- Write in the past tense.

- Plan the proportions of your story.

- Use your chronology.

- Aim for continuity, and cover all periods of your life.

CONTENT

- Give facts priority.

- Limit your 'cast list'.

- Link paragraphs and create a narrative thread.

- Include a few reflections but keep sidetracks to a minimum.

- Write to be read by another reader.

Evaluating Your Blueprint Story

After you have finished writing your blueprint story, leave it for a day or two if possible, then read it all the way through. The first time you read it, don't stop to edit or mark it – just take it all in.

How does it strike you? Does it leave you feeling excited and keen to go on to the extended narrative? Is it a shock to see your life recorded in such a few pages? Does it make you feel nostalgic or happy, or does it, perhaps, generate mixed emotions? Any or all of these feelings are good, as they imply that you've created a lively narrative which captures something of the spirit of your life. The seed is germinating, beginning to sprout, and the period of growth and flowering lies ahead.

The paradox of writing your life story is that although you may be recording what is past and gone, the act of writing it generates new life. It can help you to look forward, even though you are looking backwards when you write. It can inspire you with new ideas for things that you would like to do, and reveal threads in your life that sparkle with promise, just waiting for you to take them up again.

Working on your blueprint story

If your blueprint story doesn't raise quite this level of enthusiasm just yet, don't worry. It's a short account after all, where the main priority is to fit in the facts; so it might come across as somewhat pedestrian in style, or slightly disjointed to start with. But in either case, whether you are inspired or just moderately satisfied, do review and revise your blueprint story; this will leave the story in good shape and will also be useful practice for your full narrative.

Here are the main things you now need to do:

- Reread and edit your story.
- Make a note of events and periods you would like to expand on.
- See what themes the blueprint throws up.
- Decide on a title.
- Reflect on the experience of actually writing the story.
- Ask yourself if it is coherent to another reader.

EDITING

How much editing is needed will depend largely on you. People vary in the way they write, and you may find that because you are slow and careful, by the time you've finished, there is scarcely anything that you want to change. Or you may be someone who goes at a gallop, eager to get the material down, knowing that you will need to return to it later to tidy it up.

This project is not about setting literary standards, and you are free to work at the level which suits you. So the general rule here is to edit to a degree which brings both personal satisfaction to you and makes the text intelligible to your readers. Spelling and grammar checkers are there to help if you use word-processing software, though they need to be applied with a dose of common sense.

TIPS FOR EDITING

- Correct spelling and grammar if need be.

- Make sure the text flows easily from one sentence to another.

- Check that you have included the essential names, places and dates/periods.

- Cut unnecessary words or phrases.

- Look at the beginning and ending, making sure they are clear and strong to give weight to your narrative.

- Add in a few more reflective comments if you have the space in which to do so.

IDEAS FOR EXPANSION

As you reread your blueprint story, you may realise that there are various events, episodes and people in your life that you would like to say more about. One way of keeping tabs on all of these is to jot down words or phrases which will remind you of them; you could do this on a spare copy of your blueprint story, marking up places where you want to insert more. An easy and eye-catching way to do this is to draw a line from the relevant passage out into the margin, and write your note in a 'bubble' to remind you of the topic you plan to expand on.

It's better to wait until later to write the full text for your new themes. Although it can seem absolutely essential that you set that paragraph or story down right now so that it doesn't evaporate, it's better to focus on one task at a time – in this case editing the blueprint story. Trust to your memory: your mind is more retentive than you may give it credit for. As long as there is a note to remind you later, this prompt will usually serve as a magnet which will draw together your thoughts and ideas when you need them. And sometimes they will be all the better for having been left on the back burner for a while.

THEMES THAT EMERGE IN YOUR STORY

When you read through your blueprint story again, you may notice that it contains various themes that you were unaware of as you wrote it. These can be interesting indicators of how you approach life, and the kind of events that come your way. Sometimes it can generate a realisation that you are not entirely a victim of circumstance, and that some of the situations in which you have found yourself may have arisen out of your own desires and motivations. Are there regular patterns of change indicated, for instance (changing jobs, moving house, new relationships)? Have accidents featured prominently in your life? Are there particular themes recurring in your work and personal life (love of the unusual, taking care of others, desire for achievement and so on)? This is not to suggest that your blueprint story is a tool to use for in-depth psychological analysis, but there may be threads running through it which really do help you to see the 'storylines' of your life.

You may also find a polarisation of themes, an apparent contradiction between one urge and another, playing a leading part in your life. To give an example, I noticed how my own blueprint story revealed my dual desire both for freedom and structure. I saw by the progress of events how I often broke away from an over-restricted situation, yet some time later put myself back into a more structured framework. After some thought, I recognised this as one of my chief character traits – an urge towards independence (my mother said that I struggled to tie my shoe laces at the age of three, but cried furiously if anyone tried to help me) yet, at the same time, a desire to be secure, to have structure in my life and to be approved of by those in authority.

Often key elements of personality are constructed around this kind of polarity – elements which seem like contradictions, but which are, in fact, two sides of the same coin. It is not usually a weakness of character, but a powerful dynamic, like an electric current generated between two poles, and, as such, it can be a force which affects and even creates events in your life. Again, the aim in this context is not to try and unravel the causes of this, or to make changes to your behaviour (though understanding it may give you more choice over the decisions you take), but to witness the forces that shape your life, and to celebrate them in the life story.

DECIDING ON A TITLE

After finishing the blueprint story, your mind may well be racing with ideas for the full life story. Among these could be, perhaps, a title? Not all life stories have a title beyond a simple description, such as, 'Mary Jennifer Brown: A Life Story'. But plenty do, and it's an excellent way to allow your imagination and maybe your sense of humour to define your future narrative. A good title will also help to give your story instant appeal, and possibly extend its circle of readers beyond your loyal friends and family. If you were visiting someone's house, for instance, and saw on the coffee table a copy of 'The Life and Times of Alfred Underwood', you might hesitate to pick it up. The colourful travel magazine on the same table would definitely seem more entertaining. But if the memoir was called, 'Galloping Down the Old Kent Road: The Life and Times of a London Costermonger' you would seize it at once – or at least, I would!

So if you think you'd like your story to have a title, and you don't already have one, it's time to start thinking one up.

TIPS FOR FINDING A TITLE

- Allow yourself plenty of time to decide on the title, as the right one can take a while to emerge.

- Jot down all your ideas, even if some of them seem silly or strange at first. You may find later that one of them slots into place, or acts as a stepping stone to your final choice.

- By all means, use humour, but be wary of a play on words or an allusion which might not be understood by future generations.

- Try out your proposed title on a few friends to make sure that it's clear and appropriate.

- Don't panic if nothing strikes you for a while – working further through the different aspects of the life story, as set out in this book, will probably stir your imagination and help to focus your ideas.

- If the title doesn't include your name, you should plan to insert it underneath as a subtitle, as it should appear on the cover or title page.

YOUR EXPERIENCE OF WRITING THE LIFE STORY

Now that you've written the first draft of your blueprint story, you may like to reflect on the experience of having done so. Did you rediscover moments of happiness or the flavour of good times from years gone by? Were there any difficult or painful moments in setting down your account? If you can, allow these experiences, both pleasurable and painful to float back into your mind now. Allow them to surface in full measure, and let the feelings to reveal their own truth; it isn't necessary to over-analyse them, only to recognise and not shy away from them.

Assimilating what might be called the emotional content of a life story is an important part of the writing process, not only to give the narrative validity, but also because this can open a door to further memories and recollections that can serve as material for it. Sometimes the process of revisiting these highly charged moments can lead to discovering buried memories, or to the fuller reality of an experience which you have glossed over.

Giving time to this way of reflection outside the actual writing sessions can be helpful, since if powerful emotions surge up at the time of writing, they can be overwhelming and hinder you in what you are trying to express. One of Britain's much-loved poets, William Wordsworth, suggested that the best writing comes from 'emotion recollected in tranquillity'.

IS YOUR WRITING COHERENT?

We've looked at the usefulness of 'writing to be read' (see p. 80). Now is the time, if you wish, to let a trusted friend read your blueprint story. Explain that this is only a first, condensed version, which will serve as a basis for your final narrative. Test it out on them, and see if there are any obvious flaws that you can remedy. Can they follow the narrative? Does it seem as though there are significant gaps? Does it engage their interest?

I have suggested passing it to a friend, rather than a relative at this stage, since anyone from your own family is inevitably going to have 'a view' (probably a strong view) on the narrative you've created. They will have their own perspective, and may well be bursting to put you right on how you *should* have portrayed the family Christmas when your father walked out. For this reason, I'd recommend that you don't show your life story to a relative until you are at, or very nearly at, the final stage of composing it. The same argument also applies to letting a spouse or long-term partner read it.

Once you have written your blueprint story, edited it and reflected upon it, you will have accomplished something very worthwhile. It's no mean achievement to have set down the story of your life, albeit in shortened form, and it's a major milestone along the way to creating your complete life story. Of course, the blueprint can also be a final destination, as mentioned earlier, if you don't have the time or opportunity to take your project further; and for those of you who do plan to continue, I hope you are now inspired by the realisation of how interesting your life is, and what you can do with it in narrative terms.

CHAPTER FIVE

The Tree of Life

Writing a full life story involves not just the personal narrative, but a sense of the family background too, and the roots from which you have come. Now that we've etched out the basic storyline, we can explore the theme of the family network, and how it can best be described in the life story. There is plenty of flexibility here, and the amount of family detail to include is very much a matter of choice. You may prefer to give just minimal details about your parents, siblings and grandparents, or you may come from a big family whose activities have played a large part in your life, and without them your story would not be complete. You might also wish to set the scene by looking further back into the past, and writing a few lines about your great-grandparents. If you can go back further still, into the realms of family history, there may be exciting stories about your ancestors which you are keen to tell.

Family history is a separate topic in its own right, and the material you use from it has to be kept in proportion with the personal story that you are going to narrate. However, it can be immensely rewarding, so we are now going to look at ways to start on your family research, if you haven't already done so, and how to use some of it in your narrative. Once again, I recommend reading and working through this chapter as a whole, so that you can look at the entire theme of family in relation to your personal life story, and then decide how you wish to move forward with it.

The Great Tree

We frequently use the phrase 'family tree', but why has the image of a tree been chosen to represent family relationships? A family tree is, in fact, one version of an ancient and universal symbol, known as the 'Tree of Life'. All over the world, there are myths and legends about a mighty tree, which represents the entire life of the universe. Very often, it is depicted as the source and home of all creatures, its roots penetrating the depths of the earth, and its branches reaching up into the highest heavens. It is also a symbol of the raw elements that combine to create and sustain life, sometimes described as earth, water, fire and air. The branches in the sky represent the air, the ground of course is the earth, and water and fire are depicted as rain and sunshine, mingling with air and earth to produce new life forms, and a green and blossoming world for all to dwell in. We humans too, are part of this great flow of life; we belong to the myriad lives that are conceived, born, matured, then ultimately received back into the greater sphere of life, back to the Tree which grows and renews itself eternally.

This image, a symbol of our common origins, helps to stretch our conception of life, and indicates that the boundaries we may perceive between ourselves and others are not as fixed as they may seem. Nothing in existence is entirely separate; we are all dependent upon one another, and on the elements of growth that sustain us. We are products of history, of time and place, and, of course, of our families and perhaps our ancestors too. All this helps to define our individual identity, and shows how it arises from one source, even though we each still have that unique kernel at the centre of our being, the essential 'I' that makes us indisputably who we are.

The Tree of Life is portrayed as immortal, and is the source, the dwelling place and the resting place of individual creatures. Sometimes human souls are seen as leaves growing on that one mighty tree, or as birds roosting there. For example, one beautiful story from the Nanai people of Siberia speaks of a heavenly tree in which all potential human souls reside as a flock of birds. If a woman dreams of a bird flying towards her, she will soon become pregnant, as it signifies that a human soul is seeking to join her. If a child dies, the family's sorrow may be eased by the knowledge that its soul will fly straight back to the shelter of that tree.

Such myths can always reveal different layers of meaning, which grow and emerge over time if we are not too fixed in our interpretations. So if you contemplate the symbol of the Tree of Life, and sow it in your mind like a seed, the chances are that it will grow and flourish there, offering further insights into the wisdom that it contains.

Try the exercise below, which will help you to allow the image of the Tree of Life to enter your consciousness and work its magic there.

Exercise: growing a Tree of Life

1. Begin in an upright, but relaxed position, breathing gently and naturally.
2. Close your eyes and allow your thoughts to settle.
3. Now visualise a huge tree that grows out of the earth up into the sky, as high as you can see. Imagine its roots too, penetrating the depths of the earth, going right down into the hidden nooks and crannies.
4. Look at the branches of the trees, and see them covered with leaves. Do you see birds on the branches, or any creatures round about the trunk of the tree or any life forms in the ground below it?
5. Now, keeping the tree image in place, let the detail develop, growing and moving as it wants to. Acknowledge the life force that you see there, and the myriad forms that it produces.

If you enjoy this exercise and find it beneficial, you can repeat it whenever you have time and opportunity, and are not actively engaged in some task. It need not necessarily be in a quiet room on your own; you can call it to mind while sitting on a bus or a train, for instance. The image may be different each time you invoke it, so observe the changes and any new aspects of it that you see.

When you have become familiar with doing this exercise, you

can, if you wish, take it one stage further and align your breathing with it. So as you breathe in, gently but deeply, see the tree growing, expanding with your breath, and reaching down into the depths as well. As you breathe out, just let the image be there in your imagination, but simply as it appears, without deliberately changing it in any way.

The benefits of this exercise are that it increases your sense of connection with Life with a big 'L'. And Life is, after all, what the life story, is about. Although it is ultimately a calming and grounding exercise, you may find it a little unsettling to start with. It triggers the awareness that your single individual life is part of something huge, bigger beyond anything you can imagine. Where are the normal boundaries? How is it that 'I' am 'I', a distinct individual, and yet I am also a part of this sphere of life? Am I just one leaf on this tree, one sole bird that has taken up residence in human form? If you allow such questions to arise, they will often lead to a new understanding, sometimes gently and slowly over a long period of time.

You may be thinking that we have digressed rather from the track of the personal life story, but I'd like to suggest that by opening yourself up to the concept of *total* life, through the medium of a powerful and ancient image, you can then focus more clearly upon your individual story. It can energise the narrative force of the life story, renewing passion for life, and encouraging you to recount the experiences you have passed through. As a simple analogy, imagine that you had been cooped up in your own home for a long time, then decided to open the door and take a stroll down the lane; you might then experience awe and delight at the world outside, which, in turn, refreshes your vision of your own living space and your pleasure at inhabiting it.

The Human Tree

Considering the greater scale of life as shown through the symbol of the Tree of Life also helps to set the scene for looking at the family tree. It should also be clear by now why we usually describe personal ancestry as a 'tree', and why it is a good image for illustrating the spread of the family over a period of time. A family tree is really just a more local and personal version of the Tree of Life, but it is also on a more manageable scale: the great Tree of Life might leave you in awe, but it does not give you a practical map with which to navigate your story, whereas the family tree can lend you support and help you to make sense of your individual life. Many societies have what are known as 'ancestor cults', in which departed relatives are seen as helping to give the current generation strength and guidance. In contemporary Western society, we don't usually come at our understanding of family in quite this way, but the family tree can, nevertheless, give us meaning and a sense of continuity through the generations.

The idea of a family tree is also matched by certain practices in indigenous and folk traditions too, some of them probably very ancient. In parts of Siberia, families choose a particular tree in the forest to symbolise their collective welfare and growth, and they tend it carefully, as the wellbeing of the tree is thought to relate directly to their own family's health and happiness. The tree in a decorative form is often chosen as a symbol of the family too; marriage chests in central Russia, for instance, used to be painted with a tree motif to represent the line of the family, and their wish to perpetuate it through this latest union of bride and groom.

So the stylised family tree as we know it, representing our family history, is just one version of an old family symbol, and one that currently serves us very well in suggesting family members past and present, and the hope of growth for the future.

Your family tree

In practical terms, it's useful to construct a family tree, if only a very simple version. We'll be tackling this a little further on (see p. 100), and even if you already have a detailed family tree, it's still worth following the exercise as it will focus your mind in a different way for the purposes of the life story. And at the end of the chapter, there is a section on family history with advice for those who would like to take this kind of research further.

To start with, here are some suggestions to help you create material for the family story, which can be integrated into your narrative:

- Write down the names of your grandparents, if you know them, and try to find them out if you're not sure.
- Think about all the relatives that you've met in your life, and list those who you would like to include.
- Cover both sides of the family – your mother's line, as well as your father's.
- Jot down any incidents you associate with them, and anything that strikes you about their character, appearance, or life history.
- Choose a relative to do a 'bubble writing' exercise for, turning your 'bubble' notes into a short account of the person.
- Consider how you want to include any siblings that you may have; make notes on your relationship with them, and on key interactions that have taken place.

NO ORDINARY FAMILY TREE?

Everyone has to have a father and a mother to get born at all, but not all of us know our biological parents. You may be adopted, have lived in care, or have one parent who died early and of whom you have no memory. In Western society, the percentage of families comprising a father, mother and children, is shrinking year by year. Many children are living with step-siblings, or experience moving between two families, when their father and mother have separated. There are now also young people growing up in families based on same-sex partnerships. However, there can be few of us who have no sense of family at all. Most of us know who we think of as family members, even if they are not all biologically related to us, and these people certainly have a place in our life story. And, depending on individual circumstances, you may have to include more than one 'family' in the narrative.

In general, even if you have had little or no contact with your biological parents, I would recommend including details of them and possibly of other members of your bloodline family, if you can. If you have no information at present, then perhaps you could research this, seeking specialist advice and help as needed. It could be helpful to indicate your line of descent in your life story, especially if you have children who may want to know their genetic inheritance. This can be painful in some instances, but keep in mind how things change: people of a previous generation often desperately tried to conceal the fact that they were illegitimate, whereas nowadays this carries little, if any, stigma at all. The facts of life that you may try to cover up now – those that make you ashamed or angry – are likely to seem far more acceptable to a later generation.

Once you have worked out the information you want to include on your biological family, you may prefer to concentrate on writing more about the family that you *did* grow up in (if these are not one and the same). And even if this is a sticking point and you did not have a family in the usual sense of the word, you might have lived in a community that was your 'family', or had friends who formed your 'tribe'. If you can describe this, it will help to provide a sense of family in your narrative, even if you decide to keep it brief.

THE DNA TREE

New opportunities are springing up nowadays for us to trace our genetic roots still further back via DNA testing. If you are keen to follow this kind of 'Who do you think you are?' quest, then it could be an interesting way to map out your background. But make sure that you fully understand the testing process and what information it can give you. I signed up for a DNA project of which the overall aim was to map the migrations of peoples around the world. However, although I had hoped that it would show me how strong my Celtic roots were (or weren't), I was disappointed to find that the results simply linked me to the majority of inhabitants of the British Isles, who had arrived there on the wave of early human migration from Africa through Western Europe. So if you are paying for testing, be sure to investigate exactly what kind of report you are likely to get, and whether it can tell you anything about the more recent past, rather than your origins in pre-history.

Stories turn up in magazines and newspapers too, about individuals who opted to test whether they were in fact biologically related to other members of their family, and who then suffered considerable upset and trauma on discovering that they were not who they thought they were. Such accounts suggest that you should be cautious not only about overgeneralised DNA mapping, but also the very specific tests that could make or break family relationships.

Weaving in Your Family Story

On the information trail

Collecting material on your family for your life story is an excellent idea, and we'll shortly consider approaches for this. As with any writing project, you will probably gather far more information than you can realistically use. Enjoy the gathering process, but you will need to be prepared to hone it down and be very selective about the elements you include, for the sake of your overall narrative. It is, after all, *your* life story and this needs to be the predominant theme. Here are some tips:

- Ask your relatives for sight of any mementos, papers and photos that they might have. You may find it helpful to make copies or take photos of these, if permitted.
- Consider organising your family material and information into a separate folder, and keeping it as a separate resource, valuable in its own right. It could even act as a family archive. If various items need to be kept separately, in photo albums, for instance, then keep a log of the resources that you have, and where they can be found.
- It is always worth saving surplus material from one project to use in the next. Once you have completed your life story project, you might be inspired to write a family history or an account of your family in more recent times.

What the family story can mean to you

In your life story narrative, you may well use only a fraction of the resources you have available, but the value of preparing these is immense. Looking through family mementos, studying photos with a fresh eye, researching family history and chatting to relatives can give you a whole new outlook on your family background. It is the place from whence you came, the nest you flew from, and recognising its meaning in your life can give you a new realisation about who you are as an individual, and how you may have been influenced by the family in your life choices.

These influences can even go back to ancestors that you have never met. My main work has always been as a writer, but I do have a love of trading, and I have run two shops in my life, one selling vintage clothes, and the other Russian arts and crafts. Yet I have always recognised that being a shopkeeper is not my vocation, more of an intermittent urge. I was always puzzled as to where this impulse could be coming from, but when I started investigating my mother's family history, I discovered that I come from a line of village shopkeepers on my great-grandmother's side! At least as early as the eighteenth century, they were trading in the little town of Hemyock, in Devon, as butchers, grocers and tailors. Then my great-great grandmother began to make and sell butter on her own initiative, and built up her business into a thriving dairy, which expanded to become the biggest in the whole area.

Once I knew this part of my family background, my question was answered, and I was able to see my urge to trade as something natural, something in the blood that would probably fire me up from time to time. What this means now is that I can go with it if and when I want to; I can use the energy of the family drive if I like, but it doesn't need to drive me, nor does it have to obscure my primary vocation as a writer.

This is just one example of the surprising discoveries that you can make about your family. Some may be joyful, others uncomfortable, but they are likely to be meaningful to you and potentially good material for your life story. Most people that I have spoken to find researching their families of enormous interest, an inspiring quest that they become passionate about. Indeed, the real danger is that you could get totally absorbed by this, and tempted away from the main task of writing your own life story!

Tip:
Although you will want to enter the past
in your imagination when you research your family
background, keep a balance by having plenty of
activities and interests in the present too.
Don't look back for too long.

Where and how to include your family story

Right from the outset, it pays to think where in your narrative you will want to place the family material, and how. Remember, as always, your life story is about you, and it's you that your readers are interested in. So use your family background chiefly as it is relevant to you. Here are some key tips:

- Don't open your life story with a detailed account of your parents or ancestors, but do mention them in the early pages.
- Weave in details about your family as and when you can from then on, but keep your own story predominant.
- Do give some names and dates, but keep the narrative going; you can always create a separate family chronology to place at the beginning or end of the life story.
- If you know the history of a particular branch of your family, you could write it up as a short narrative in its own right, which will be easy to insert at a suitable point in the life story. Use any themes or storylines which are prominent (see opposite for an example).

WRITING A BRIEF FAMILY HISTORY

Before moving on to creating a narrative about your immediate family and its context, you might like to consider writing up an account based on your family history, perhaps from an earlier period, if you have enough information. You will probably need to be selective, and to choose just one or two interesting threads to follow.

Here is a fictitious example of how such a short family history narrative could be created, revolving around a particular theme. It stands in its own right, and could easily be slotted into a written narrative or a ring binder.

> The Merrivales were seafaring folk whose marine ancestry stretched back to at least the sixteenth century, when Percival Merrivale signed up as a sailor on the *Betsy* on a trading voyage to the East. Descendant Horace Merrivale fought in the Battle of Trafalgar, and in the nineteenth century there were several prominent seagoing merchants in the family. One of them did well enough to build himself a mock-Gothic mansion overlooking the Bristol Channel, on whose tower he ran up a flag whenever he spied one of his own ships coming into port. The urge to go to sea carried on further down through the generations, influencing my maternal grandmother, who was a keen yachtswoman. It is possibly expended now. My father was a naval officer, but none of us since, nor our children, has shown any interest in following him. We prefer watching from the quayside!

Picking on one theme from the family story creates a good framework, and even quite simple facts sound more interesting when embedded in this way. The sea, sailors, distant lands, old trading routes and battles all stir the imagination and entice the reader to speculate on the lives of the people mentioned. Most of us have interesting storylines running through our families, and they need not relate to people who were famous or rich.

USING A PREFACE AND APPENDICES TO ADVANTAGE

The beginning and end of a life story are great places to include extra material, lists and chronologies. Any time that you find yourself perplexed as to how you can integrate some of the more information-heavy material into your narrative, consider making it into a separate page or section for this purpose. For example:

- A 'cast list' of everyone who makes an appearance in your life story, with a few words to identify and describe each person.

- A chronology of your own life.

- A recent family chronology, or family-history chronology.

- The family tree.

Exercise: writing a narrative about your immediate family

This exercise focuses chiefly on your family context as you know it, and the aim is to write up an account of your immediate origins.

Start by constructing a simple family tree. To do this, write out the names of your paternal and maternal great-grandparents, if you know them, as well as those of your grandparents and your parents. Just leave spaces or blank boxes if there are any gaps in your knowledge.

It helps to arrange these on the page so that you can see the lines of descent. One way to do this is to work vertically down the page, with your great-grandparents at the top (eight of them, in four sets of couples) and lines descending from them to the four grandparents, then to your parents and, from them, two lines which converge in the middle of the page on you. Add any siblings alongside your own name, but don't include aunts and uncles.

Now you are going to use this family tree as the basis for a short narrative. A suggested length is between 150 – 300 words for now. The end product may be useful for inserting into your life story as it is, or you may choose to use extracts from it here and there. You can also expand on it later if you wish.

Think about each side of the family in turn: starting with your mother's side, for instance, write a brief account of your maternal great-grandparents if you know something about them. Continue with your mother's parents, then describe your mother's early life before she met your father. Then do the same thing with your father's side.

Now your two parents are set in context, and the time has come for them to meet. The subject of the next paragraph or two that you'll write is their life before you were born. You may find the following questions helpful:

- How did they meet?
- What kind of a courtship and wedding did they have?
- Where did they live?
- What work were they doing?
- What sort of lifestyle did they have?

Next, announce your own appearance on the scene: when and where were you born?

List any other children that your parents had (including any step-brothers or stepsisters). Try and weave all of this into a few sentences.

The next section involves working in pairs to write up a family story. If you are working on your own, you can if you wish move on to the Family History section later in this chapter on p. 108. However, I would suggest that you read through what follows in the pair exercise, as you'll find examples of stories, tips for framing your narrative and also answers to possible questions that may come up as you develop your family story further.

Exercise: family-story interviews (working with a friend or in pairs)

A really enjoyable way of creating this narrative is to work with a friend, or, if you are in a writing group, to work in pairs. The whole exercise will take around one hour. However, it's easy to split it into two parts, each taking about half an hour.

First of all, you should each complete the simple family tree on your own, as described above. Then take it in turns to conduct a ten-minute interview with each other.

When you're ready, take your positions either sitting opposite or at an angle to each other, so that you can glance at each other's faces. Have a clock or watch handy, to check the time allowed. Keep strictly to ten minutes! It is actually more fun – and more productive – to contain it all within a short space of time. You can set an alarm or beeper if you like.

If you start as the first interviewer, be prepared to take notes as you go. Imagine, if you like, that you are writing a short article profiling the family background of a celebrity or even just someone in the local news. You'll want to get the facts down, but also to make it interesting in terms of the character of the person you're interviewing.

If you are the first interviewee, enjoy your moment of glory. You don't need to take notes, but answer questions as accurately as you can, and don't talk for too long in response to any one of them.

ORDER OF QUESTIONS

Here is a suggested order for the first set of interview questions, designed to fill in the basic information about the family background. (Make sure that you allow enough time to ask some from the next set too.)

1. Ask your interviewee for their full name and place and date of birth.
2. Ask about the background of their mother and their father – and their own childhood and parents.
3. Ask if anything is known about the great-grandparents, or if there is anything else from further back that your interviewee would like to mention.

4. Bring the interview back to the present generation by asking about any brothers and sisters they might have.

Once you have completed this, you can move on to fill out the account with a few personal questions. Here are some examples:

- What kind of an education did you have?
- What work or profession did you take up?
- Did you marry and have children?
- Where have you lived during your life?
- Have you travelled much?
- Are there any major events in your life that you'd like to mention?

DOS AND DON'TS FOR THE INTERVIEWER

Do move the interview on if one answer is taking too long; as the interviewer you need to keep an eye on the time, but **do** also allow brief hesitations, which often lead to interesting new revelations.

Do make eye contact frequently, but **don't** stare at the other person, which can be off-putting.

Don't interrupt unless you have to; mostly keeping quiet is best, with just an appreciative nod or 'Mm,' to encourage the interviewee.

Do frame your questions as clearly and as simply as you can, and only ask one at a time.

Don't push the interviewee further than they want to go along a particular line of enquiry. This is not the place to dredge up really sensitive material.

Don't be too intense. The exercise is designed to be friendly and fun.

Do keep your brief in mind, and try and complete all stages of the questions in order so that you'll have a rounded story.

WRITING IT UP

The next phase is to write up this first interview, and each of you will do this – both interviewer and interviewee will write an account based on the answers to the questions that have just been raised. Allow fifteen minutes for this part of the exercise.

If you were the interviewer, write your account in the third person: e.g. 'Luke's family came originally from Manchester, and his parents met at art college in the 1960s.' Use the notes you made to help you.

If you were the interviewee, write in the first person, 'I', and base the account on the information that you gave during the interview. Resist the temptation to fill it out with other details and stories that you didn't have the chance to mention. It's a useful exercise to base it on what you told your interviewer, and you can always add more later on.

Once again, keep strictly to time by the clock.

When the time is up, if you are going to do both interviews in this session, move on to the second one, reversing the roles. However, if you are planning to split the exercise into two sittings, move on now to the 'Feedback' session (see p. 107).

Change positions by swapping chairs, which helps to create the sense of taking up a new role, and begin the second interview. This should be followed by another fifteen-minute period for writing.

The accounts quoted below were written in class at summer school, to a strict time limit. I have chosen extracts which are not necessarily perfect or complete examples of 'how to do it', but they do show the way in which essential elements of the family story can be captured. Here is part of an account written by Ruth, as the 'interviewer' in this pairs exercise (names and places have been changed).

> Andrew's mother's family came from Portsmouth. She was called Erica Alveston. She had a very strong character, and was quite a driver; Andrew thinks that she motor-raced a bit. In the First World War, she worked in a canteen, and in the Second she joined the WAAFS. He was very fond of her. Her own mother was Irish.

His father was in the Navy and the army during the two world wars, and he farmed before working in an advertising agency . . . Andrew's childhood was spent with his two sisters in a house near Canterbury with a nice garden, a tennis court, a nanny and male servants who came from an institution. He thinks his parents met when they were quite young. His mother had two brothers, one killed in the First World War, and one who served in the Indian army.

This is a very serviceable account, which sets down the bare bones of the story well. There is certainly plenty of scope for elaborating later on: a mother who was a racing driver; servants who came from an institution? Those are details which set the imagination going and we'd definitely like to hear more! Andrew might find it useful to develop his narrative using Ruth's account too, as it brings out the contours and the significant elements of his story.

Tip:
When another person writes up
your family story, this can highlight details
which you might have considered unimportant or
uninteresting, but which will be intriguing for others
to read about. Ask them for a copy of their
account, so that you can use it in conjunction
with your own if you want to extend
your family narrative

Sophia wrote up her own story after she was interviewed. This is an extract from her narrative, showing how her family story crosses international boundaries, and includes culture clashes and a hint of wider events being played out on the world stage. Once again, it gives us plenty of food for thought, and opportunities for further storytelling. (Names and some places have been changed.)

I was born in Hampstead, London, in 1930, the first daughter of Alanna (X) from Moravia and George (X) of Hampstead.

My parents had met in Avignon, France, in 1924 while on a 'grand tour', my mother being six years older than my young and very handsome father. The English family were against the marriage but my father was obstinate, and they finally married in 1929. I was born a year later, and have one sister, Catherine, born in 1933.

My mother's father was a shoemaker who married a young Czech woman who was in service in Salzburg, but she became pregnant and came back to Moravia. They had a son born in 1897 and then my mother, born in 1899, and two more children, one of whom died.

George's parents were strong Methodists. My father's father was a well-to-do businessman from a good family; they had eight children, one of whom died, leaving three sons, and four daughters. My father was the eldest son, born in 1905.

My mother started life in the UK as a language teacher, but when she had two children, my father left us. I was aged six. My mother was unhappy and tried to go back to Moravia to live, but was told in September 1938 that she must go back to England.

My father had political ambitions, and tried to get into Parliament for the Commonwealth Party. Later he founded an organisation called 'Justice'.

Overcoming personal reserve and respecting family privacy

Sophia's background is fascinating, and she is a fluent writer but, in spite of this, she needed our encouragement in class to set it all down and to believe that it was of interest. Many people are brought up with the idea that it is not acceptable to talk or write too much about themselves and, in this case, they may feel resistant to doing so. But in order to write a life story, you have to break through any social conditioning which decrees that your personal story is not of value, whether this stems from a deeply rooted national trait (such as the typical British stiff upper lip, especially true of an older generation), from religious or cultural heritage or, perhaps, from a family's desire to start anew and not revisit the past. Even if such principles come from your parents' or grandparents' generation, you may still be affected by them. But in recognising them for what they are, you have a choice as to whether you want to overcome these barriers in the interests of writing a life story.

This is not to say that you should trample ruthlessly on family feelings. There may be ethical choices to make along the way: do you reveal that Granny Maureen was the illegitimate daughter of an Irish servant girl and an unknown father, instead of the well-brought up daughter of respectable teachers that she always claimed to be? Research tools are very powerful now, and censuses and documents that are freely available online can demolish family myths in a short space of time. In such a case, you would need to think carefully about the implications, especially, of course, if the person in question is still alive. However, even when they have passed on, you might still choose to respect their sensitivities and leave out certain pieces of information. I would not recommend overtly perpetuating the myth by pretending it is the truth, if you know differently, but sometimes a graceful omission may be the best option.

In overcoming your reserve, be very careful of including anything that could lead to family conflict when your story is read, or even to libel action. It's easy to write something in the heat of the moment and to regret it later, so cast a cool eye over your life story before circulating it. Be aware too, that even though you may only plan to hand it to a few close family members and friends, you are likely to end up showing it to a much wider range of people, and in any case, word will get round about its contents if they are inflammatory! Make your choices wisely about what to include, without stifling your feelings as they emerge in your writing.

FFEDBACK

Feedback from this exercise can be as long or as short as you want; it is often rewarding to extend it in a group situation, where some or all of the participants can be invited to read back the accounts written, and discussion can follow. It can be especially interesting to hear how the accounts of the interviewer and the interviewee differ.

If you are just working as a pair of friends, read what you have written out loud to one another. When both sets of narratives have been written and read out, you may like to discuss the experience. Some useful questions are:

- Did you learn anything new about yourself?
- Did you find it easy to convert the other person's information into a narrative?
- How did you feel about being interviewed?
- Do you think you can fit this into your life story?

Researching Family History

Once upon a time, doing your family history meant traipsing off to obscure record offices and poring over dusty volumes in the hope of finding a trace of your ancestors. It wasn't something that most people considered doing, particularly if they were young and scornful of the past, as compared with the exciting present.

In the late 1960s, I remained aloof while my father devoted the first years of his retirement to researching his ancestry. This took him off to Dublin's record offices and into the Irish countryside, where he trudged down country lanes to find traces of a lost past in the form of surviving elderly relatives, and ruined country mansions once inhabited by his family. It meant he was cloistered in his study for hours at a time, studying ancient tomes in a fug of pipe smoke, clacking away on the typewriter and swapping news with fellow researchers. At the time, I remained uninterested in the portraits of ancient relatives who now glared down from every wall of the house. What relevance did it have to me? I enjoyed some of the stories he recounted, especially the one about my two-times great-grandmother, the thirteen-year-old heiress who eloped with her cousin to France, pursued by a posse of alarmed relatives, but by and large I said a polite thank you when he gave me copies of his latest findings, and stuffed the rest into a file for perusal later – much, much later, as it turned out.

It took another forty years before I too became hooked, and a few years ago, I took a day course on researching family history online, with the idea of investigating my mother's side. This opened the door to the past for me, and within a few hours I had plunged into a new world of silk weavers, miners, postmistresses and Baptist ministers. The Internet has revolutionised family history research, and can yield a staggering amount of information. Although good research may still include personal visits to record offices, archives and churches, the Internet, with its numerous websites devoted to family history, and many archive records online, can supply much of what is needed to explore your ancestry in a fraction of the time. A full inventory of these is beyond the scope of this book, but there is a selected list of websites in the Resources section (see p. 201), and a few useful tips on general family history below.

Discovering an ancestor

The way I have chosen to illustrate the process is by showing how I discovered one of my own ancestors, a project which grew in its own organic and often surprising way through explorations and personal contacts, as well as the use of standard resources. In the end, I believe that family history is not so much about filling in the gaps on the family tree, but about the process of revealing the story and finding out what it means to you.

I first found my three-times great-grandfather, Edward Owens, through an email from America. This turned out to be from another descendant who was also researching the family history, and who had found me through a family-history website where we had both uploaded our family trees. We discovered that our great-grandfathers David and John were brothers. Both emigrated to the USA, but whereas John stayed there, David (my great-grandfather) returned home to the UK, so that his son Bernard, my mother's father, was born and brought up in England. The Owens were, unsurprisingly, Welsh in origin, but

I knew little more than that until my new-found American cousin supplied some information from an old family bible. Often, those who emigrated treasured their family mementos more than those who stayed at home, as precious links with the folk left behind. This bible was inscribed, as was the general custom then, with the births and deaths of family members, and it listed the name of David's grandparents as Edward and Maria.

I checked the censuses for Wales in 1841 and 1851, and found Edward Owens and his wife Maria living in the little village of Abbeycwmhir in mid-Wales. I noticed that Edward was listed as a Chelsea Pensioner, which implied he had been a soldier, and a bell started to ring – I'd inherited some notes from my uncle, which mentioned an old family story in which one of our ancestors had fought at the battle of Waterloo, and been wounded there. This would be about the right period for Edward. So the next trail I followed was to check up on the records at the National Archives, to see if I could trace him as a soldier in the Napoleonic Wars.

It took me nearly a whole day to scan through the entries, but I finally found him. And on his discharge record, dated 1816, he suddenly came to life for me, for it gave a description of what he looked like: five-foot nine inches tall, hair brown, eyes grey, complexion brown. And his occupation was that of 'cordwainer' or shoemaker. I learnt that he suffered chronic hepatitis after fighting in the Walcheren campaign (an ill-judged expedition into the Low Countries which left half the army very ill). This man had become very real to me.

A trip to Abbeycwmhir followed, where I was amazed at the remoteness and beauty of this small settlement, which was, incidentally, once home to one of the largest abbeys in Europe. I looked for the cottage where Edward and Maria had lived, and talked to locals to find out some of the stories of the area. Later, I located other villages and towns roundabout, where their children, including my two-times great-grandfather (also called Edward) had lived, and I started to get to know the terrain, including bustling Newtown, tranquil Painscastle and the Victorian respectability of Builth Wells.

I also began to understand how the storylines worked: Edward senior, back from the wars with a scanty pension and ill health, had a large family to look after. He had seen the world and fought for his country, but came back to near poverty and rural obscurity.

I found his marriage banns to Maria in 1799, and realised that neither of them could read or write; touched as I was to see their mark (a cross) on the page, I knew that they would have been held back without education. But they must have encouraged their children into education and a different life, one with more options open to them. Their eldest son Edward went to college and became a Baptist minister, an avenue leading to a new world. David, his son and my great-grandfather, also followed the calling to the ministry, and moved out of Wales, first to Devon, then to America and finally to Northamptonshire. By then, the family was well and truly mobile in a way that would have been impossible a generation earlier.

Perhaps the urge to rove was already in the family, and Edward senior fulfilled it by the only way open to him, as a soldier. His wife Maria was also a plucky woman who was prepared to expand her horizons, since one of her daughters was born in Pharo, Sicily; and she must have been stationed there with the regiment, probably following it unofficially, as some soldiers' wives did at the time.

Then it was time for me to check up on the family legend of Waterloo. I discovered that Edward was nowhere near Waterloo, but that he was awarded a medal at the battle of Corunna in 1809. He was a foot soldier in the 81st regiment, which bore the brunt of the fighting. And, at last, I located his death certificate; Maria had already died, and Edward, then residing at an inn in the nearby town of Rhyader, passed away two days before Christmas in 1854. His life story was over; he had learnt a trade, brought up a large family, survived battles, ill health and poverty, and lived on till his late seventies, apparently undaunted. The cause of death was simply given as 'old age'.

So through this research, I now have a sense of who Edward Owens was, and where he came from. I have been moved and affected by his life, and I can now understand something of the story that has unfolded in the subsequent generations of the family. There are still many questions to explore, but fresh information keeps turning up, and I'm now in touch with several more descendents in the USA, Wales and England, and have met a number of them. We have discovered a shared inheritance, and a tendency to gravitate towards music, languages and teaching. We've swapped stories, enjoyed much laughter and experienced some poignant moments, too. The past has, to some extent, come back to life in the present, and I think we all feel the richer for it. Even though Edward was born over two hundred years ago, his life has touched ours.

This was the process of 'discovering' Edward Owen, and it's easy to see how the details about his life could now be written up as a short cameo portrait of the man, and the influence he had on the family. You may want to write something similar for your own life story: descriptions of relatives that you have known, or ancestors from the past, who have made your family what it is and who have thus affected your story.

Family history resources

The following are some of the main paths to explore when working on family history:

1. Websites for viewing the census, finding birth, marriage and death certificate information (BMD) and other information, e.g. (as in my case, above) the Medal Roll for Corunna. Examples are www.ancestry.com and www.findmypast.com.
2. Family history forums and websites where you can communicate with other people researching their own family, and possibly connect with descendants from your tree with whom you can swap information, e.g. www.genesreunited.co.uk.
3. Local record offices; in my case, I looked up the parish entry for the marriage of Edward and Maria and the births of some of their children.
4. Public record repositories, such as the National Archives in Kew in the UK, where I found Edward's discharge report.

5. Family stories, such as the 'legend' of the ancestor who fought at Waterloo. Although they may be part myth, nevertheless there is often a grain of truth that can lead to exciting discoveries, in this instance that my ancestor was decorated for military service.

6. Visits to the locality. These can give you a strong sense of place and of tuning in to the life that your ancestors lived there. You may also be able to see houses they inhabited, schools they attended and so on.

I'll give more leads and suggestions for exploring your family history on p. 114, but first, here is a more personal and imaginative exercise that you might like to try. It follows on from the Tree of Life visualisation on p. 91. In this one, you are going to reflect upon your own particular family tree.

Exercise: contemplating your family tree

Close your eyes, and 'see' your family tree in whatever form you have created it, even if it is only a very simple diagram with just a couple of generations on it. See where you yourself are positioned on it, then acknowledge and name your immediate family – parents, siblings and your own children – as relevant. Add in any aunts and uncles, then go further back to your grandparents. If you are also familiar with the names of great-uncles and great-aunts or great-grandparents, proceed to acknowledge these relatives too.

Whenever the inclusion of new names becomes too much to keep in mind, or when you run out of definite information, then just allow the image of the family tree to grow in your mind, expanding backwards in time through the generations of the past, and across to include other branches of the family. Let it become a tree now, rather than a diagram, a huge tree, which reaches higher and wider than you can see. It doesn't matter if the image is indistinct or fuzzy. Keep a sense of all the people who have made up, and continue to make up this tree. You might perceive them as little sparks of life, little flickers of energy or perhaps even hear a kind of background 'chatter' that denotes their presence.

When you have had enough, acknowledge your link to this tree, thank your family and forbears and let the image dissolve. Don't try to hang on to it as you open your eyes. Making contact with the family in this way can be powerful, and should only be of limited duration. Make sure you are fully back in the normal world.

You may find that this exercise starts to give you a sense of your family as a living being, where past and present both exist, and with perhaps a hint of the future too. Keep it to a simple experiment, however, and bear in mind that whatever you experience or perceive may be of a symbolic nature, rather than the literal or absolute truth.

First steps to family-history research

The following suggestions should help set you on your way with your family research. For those in the first list you will need to use a computer, but the second list is useful either as an adjunct to your online research, or in its own right if you cannot use or don't have access to a computer. (See also Resources, p. 200, for specific recommendations.) In addition, you should speak to relatives if you can, and check out any mementos or family heirlooms.

ONLINE
- Consider taking a short course or an online tutorial about researching your family history on the Internet.
- Acquire an up-to-date software programme for recording your family tree.
- Join a website such as Genes Reunited, where you may 'meet' other people researching a branch of your family.
- Log on to one or more general family history research sites, to check out census results, BMD registration and so on.
- Look out for free trial subscription offers which may allow you to access all the records available on the website for a limited time. You may also get free access to certain sites from a library computer.

- Seek out some of the more specific sites that may be useful for your project, for example, those dealing with railway ancestors, military history, workhouse registers and so on.
- Explore national and regional archives which have indexed their collections on the Internet.
- Try general Internet searches (e.g. through Google) using your ancestor's name, location, etc. It is astonishing what this can throw up. Use creative combinations of keywords to hone your search.

OFFLINE
- Take a short course on researching family history.
- Sample some of the family history magazines that are now generally available – they give valuable advice and may whet your appetite for further research.
- Consider joining a family history society for the local areas you are interested in.
- Visit family history fairs to stimulate your interest, and see the related products on offer.
- Visit locations where your family or ancestors lived.
- Buy a good book on researching family history; this should give you sound information on how to trace your ancestors using archives and local records.
- Go to local or national archives to check records that are not available online.

TALK TO YOUR RELATIVES

'I wish I had talked to Uncle Bert before he died!' is a common cry. 'Now I'll never know exactly what happened to him in the war.' 'Why did my great-aunt Susan leave home so young? I could have asked her that myself, but now it's too late.'

Don't be caught out! Talk to any living relatives from an older generation while there is still a chance to record memories, check dates and ask leading questions. Take a voice recorder if you can or write everything down. Then treasure your findings as gold.

If most of your older relatives have died, there may still be papers, letters and photos kept by other members of the family that you can look at. My last surviving aunt, from a Swedish family herself, had faithfully kept all my uncle's family mementos after he died. When she heard I was researching the family history, she invited me to come and look through them. I was thrilled to discover letters written by my grandparents and photographs of my great-grandparents, whose faces I had never seen before. Various other items, such as my grandfather's birthday book had also been preserved, and this, as well as being a wonderful keepsake, also helped to verify family dates that I was checking and point me towards finding their birth certificates.

Family mementos and treasures

Do you have any family heirlooms in the household that could give you a nugget of information about your family that would be interesting to include in a life story? Before you shake your head, think again. It need not mean diamond bracelets smuggled out of revolutionary Russia, letters of commendation from Nelson or a Saracen's sword brought back from the Crusades. In fact, many of us will have family mementos that are quite simple, lowly objects, which once belonged to older or earlier members of the family, and which genuinely do have a story to tell.

Start with your parents. Do you have any kitchen implements or tools that they owned? If so, what were they used for? Do they conjure up any memories or pictures in your mind of your parents? If yes, make a note of these. You may also have items of furniture, books or china that come from the family home, and which are so much a part of your life now that you haven't taken stock of them in terms of your family and personal past. Look at them afresh and, again, ask yourself what they are associated with.

For example: I have my mother's writing desk, and I remember clearly how she used to keep boxes of old buttons in the bottom drawer, which I loved to tip out as a child and sort through, looking for my favourite china button, made in the shape of a blue flower. The desk is still impregnated with the smell of her cigarette smoke; I can't get rid of it, and perhaps I don't really want to. I can also remember my mother telling me to keep away from her private letters kept in the 'secret' drawer of the desk (I did, so now I'll never know what they were!) and, on other occasions, how I saw her fishing in another of the drawers for scraps of knitting wool and elastic to help her with her mending on winter evenings. The memories evoked by this desk both form a connection with her and give me snippets of reminiscence that I may be able to use in my life story.

Look out for very humble objects, which you might otherwise pass over. In one group that I was working with, we were moved almost to tears when a woman brought a battered old potato peeler that had belonged to her mother. She told us stories of how hard this woman had worked to cook for her children, how she used to sit on the doorstep peeling apples for a pie and how her own children now feed and look after her in her old age.

Look around too, for objects that may come from more distant relatives, or from a previous generation. I have a carved wooden spoon sent by a great-uncle who emigrated to South Africa, for instance, and this has encouraged me to try and find out a little more about him and his work on the railways there. I also have a book about the English countryside given to me by another great-uncle, which reminds me of going for walks with him through the leafy village where he lived, and where I would linger hopefully outside the sweet shop, taking advantage of his generous nature. It's a key to my contact with him, and also a 'prompt' (see p. 40) to memories of him – the fusty bungalow, full of brightly coloured rugs that he had knotted himself and the way he always called me 'Daisy'.

And what about items that spell out your own past? In my case, it's things like my christening shawl, early school reports and a birthday card that I made for my father when I was five. The christening shawl, by the way, doesn't awaken memories of the day itself, as I was only four months old at the time, but of my mother telling me as a little girl that I had been put to sleep upstairs while the grown-ups enjoyed a party. My own christening party, and I wasn't even allowed to go to it! I was always very indignant when she told me this story.

If you are lucky, you may have old toys, childhood books and maybe even bundles of love letters, which will all open up memories to earlier parts of your life. Try the bubble-writing exercise (see p. 12) if there are one or two items in particular that arouse a number of associations and memories, and include the passages in your story.

While you are writing your life story, there are also opportunities for working on what may be the heritage of the future. If you have the time, it's worth combing through your possessions, and making an inventory of any items which have their own story. Write a list of what they are and brief notes of what they mean to you. Take digital photos of them if you can, and create a record for future generations, which may be deeply appreciated.

CHAPTER SIX

Building Your Life Story: Robot and Dragon

I once knew a talented musician, who played the piano and composed for it too. One night, I dreamt that I saw him standing by a pool, watching a struggle between two figures who were immersed in the water. To my surprise, I saw that the battle was between a robot and a dragon. I couldn't understand the dream, and asked a friend who was wise in such matters to interpret it for me.

'Well,' he said, 'It's all about the creative process, isn't it? That's the pool. Then you've got to have the dragon, the fire and inspiration, but you have to have the robot too, the repetitive side. Pianists have to practise their scales for hours a day, and composers need to work with the laws of harmony. Of course it's a struggle, combining them!'

So creativity needs both of these elements – the fiery imagination and the endless, almost mechanical attention to detail and technique. And writing a life story is no different. It too needs both the robot and the dragon; although it's factually based, it is a creative process, and needs both imagination and skill. Sometimes you let loose the dragon, so that the words flow and the stream of thoughts and memories take you where they will; sometimes the robot predominates, and it's the structure and style and writing technique that need your attention.

The path taken in this book takes you along both routes, so that you'll be engaging imagination and emotions, as well as learning techniques for developing control over style and structure. It aims to give you confidence in summoning and handling both the dragon and the robot. At times, they may even do battle before your eyes, as in my dream. But that's the creative process at work, and it would be a dull task if there were no challenge in it!

In this chapter, we'll consider the various components that make up a life story, and how best to structure them, and techniques to give your writing an interesting texture, plenty of lively colour and a polished style. There will also be guidelines to help you plan your extended life story presentation, and to keep the project manageable. So you might call this a robot's chapter, as it's mainly about technique and structure, but there is still plenty of room here for the dragon to brighten and enhance the work with its fire and its powers. Within every robot lurks a dragon – and vice versa, perhaps!

Planning a Life Story

You could just sit down and start to write your life story without any planning and without any specific idea as to what you would like it to contain. After all, it's *your* life. What you want to say about it will surely come to you as you go along.

Maybe. If you are a writer of genius, perhaps it'll be a runaway bestseller. Or, if you have a brilliant subconscious, the kind that does all your organising for you, you can simply follow its dictates. But most people, even experienced writers, do not fall into those categories, and many would-be life story writers have never tackled a length of narrative before that could easily extend to fifty or a hundred pages. So for the vast majority, figuring out an approach and the right ingredients in advance is vital and will help you to:

- Select what you need from all the material and memories that you have.

- Develop your story as narrative.
- Create a balanced and rounded account.
- Produce a story that other people will want to read.
- See the meaning that your life has, both to yourself and to others.
- Bring in other themes, arguments and issues from the basis of a sound structure.

Contents plan

When you prepare to write anything, from an essay to a full-length book, the normal approach is to draft a plan of its contents. This could be a list of chapters and what goes into them, or perhaps, in this case, sections and themes, laid out in the order that you will write them. The synopsis, as this is usually known, sets out the structure of the narrative, and acts as a map that will help to guide you through the actual task of writing itself.

I find that creating a synopsis for anything that I write is a very important stage in the process. It draws together my thoughts and gives me a concrete basis to work from. It's also a good check to see if my ideas are likely to work when put into a larger framework.

By now, you will probably have gathered enough material to give you a good idea about the form you want to present your story in (written narrative, ring binder, etc. – see pp. 28–38), the span of life that this will cover and the main events and periods that you'll write about. You may also have decided whether you want the story to develop chronologically, or whether you will take themes for the different sections. So you can now begin to place these in order.

Start by giving each chapter or section a number and a name. For example: 'Chapter One – Childhood' or 'Section Three – Raising a Family'. You can always think of snappier titles later on. You may find it easier to draft the full list of chapters/sections first, then add notes about their contents. So for the first example, you might write:

Chapter One – Childhood
My earliest memory (in the garden) – first school (Whitewood Primary) – childhood friends (Ken, Maggie) – family holidays (Margate, Barmouth).

When presenting a synopsis to a publisher, it has to be in a fuller form, and written so that a third party can understand it, but in the context of a life story, if you are the only person who will use the notes, you may find it easier just to write enough for your own reference.

HOW MANY CHAPTERS OR SECTIONS SHOULD THERE BE?
This depends partly on the nature of your project, and how you plan to organise it. Overall, the contents plan should provide a framework, which will help to make the life story coherent both to you and your readers.

For a written narrative, between six and ten chapters or sections works well – this is enough to give you a framework, but not so much that you risk setting a brief which could be hard to fulfil. The length of each could be anything from three or four pages upwards – using the word 'chapter' doesn't condemn you to writing a lengthy tome!

For a ring binder, or any type of presentation which won't necessarily be read from beginning to end in the same way, you could have more themed sections than this, for the reader to dip in and out of. You may also want to add more sections as you go along, as this kind of life story can be somewhat organic in growth. Even for this approach, however, it's helpful to lay out your first plan, either with your main themes, or with a chronological structure.

The Seven Key Components of a Life Story

Now that you have your life story plan under way, we can look further at how it is actually constructed in terms of its components, of which there are seven that are fundamental in writing an interesting, comprehensive and readable narrative. They are as follows:

1. Chronology
2. Characters
3. Context
4. Events and incidents
5. Summaries
6. Questions
7. A clear beginning and end

These seven ingredients are the all-important building blocks for your story, and they form a solid structure for it. Although we have already looked at some of these elements individually, considering them now as a set, and how to include all of them in the right proportions, will provide the means to fashion a well-crafted story. They are the seven pillars which will support your creation.

1. Chronology

Drawing up a chronology of your life helps you to plan the progress of your narrative, and ensures that you don't miss out anything important. It offers a sense of continuity which can help to sustain the momentum of your story. And, as mentioned in Chapter Two, it can also highlight the different phases of life, the lean and the fat years in terms of clusters of events and important experiences. These contours can act as a guide in choosing how much you want to write about each period of your life.

Chronology is, in one sense, the life story itself, which is usually told through the passing of the years, either from birth to the present moment, or for a chosen time span from your life. However, you can also use the chronology as a frame of reference in the background, rather than sticking to it literally. This allows you to move backwards and forwards in time at certain points in your narrative, which can bring a lively touch to the story. For instance, your opening paragraphs or pages might be set in the present, and from there you could move back to your early years. Here's a fictitious example of how this can be done:

I am sitting by the window looking out over the playing fields of the local school. There's a football game in progress, and I can see one of my grandsons, James, playing in goal. His brother Luke is probably sitting at his desk struggling with the maths that he finds so frustrating, or perhaps drawing maps for geography with coloured pencils, which he loves. I have four grandchildren altogether, and am lucky enough to have them living nearby. We all live in or around Rugby, in Warwickshire. My son Toby is the boys' father, and daughter Angela has two lively girls aged six and ten. My other daughter, Denise, sadly died of leukaemia when she was only twenty, and we miss her very much. I'm a widow now, but was very happily married to Anthony for over forty years. I have a small but warm house, full of the treasures we bought together on our travels; we were early backpackers, and found our way to Peru and Nepal before it was fashionable to do so.

But let me start at the beginning. I was born April Jane Anderson on – yes, you've guessed it – April 1st 1935. My mother said that she could see the trees in full flower outside when she was in labour, and decided that if it was a girl, she'd call me something to remember the beautiful spring day. Thank goodness she didn't choose Blossom!

You can see from this that it's very easy to create a 'here and now' opening to your story. Or you might choose something more dramatic; later in the book, we'll be looking at life-changing events (see pp. 131–133), and perhaps one of these might feature at the start of your story. Switching the chronology around can be hard to handle if done to any great extent, but is very effective used in moderation. If you are not sure about trying this though, stay with the usual sequence of birth onwards. Later on, when you've laid out the whole of the narrative, you may find that you can successfully juggle the order in a couple of places.

Characters

You are the leading character in your life story, so ensure that your voice and your story predominate, and that your own experiences form the main narrative thread. Enjoy the chance to star in your own story! However, don't take this to extremes, like an acquaintance of mine who begins every sentence in his 'round robin' Christmas letter with 'I', and never mentions his wife, or anyone else for that matter. Focusing exclusively on yourself can create the impression of a cold and selfish person.

Of course there will be others in the story too, so draw up a cast list of the characters who you plan to include (see p. 76). This is likely to be not only relatives, but also, for instance, friends, teachers and colleagues who have played a significant part in your life. Be selective; you will not be able to include everybody, so decide who are the major and who the minor players, and put brackets around those on the list who are unlikely to get a look-in. Keep your original list, however, because you may find that when you've completed the first draft of the narrative, you can sprinkle in a few more mentions of meaningful encounters, like adding a little salt and pepper to the final dish.

As you write your story, make sure that each new character is clearly introduced into the story when he or she first appears. Say who any relatives are, and don't overload the reader with too many names in a short space of time. Bring people in gradually, if you can. And bring them to life; even a short description can make all the difference. 'Uncle Bert often came on holiday with us,' tells the reader nothing, whereas, 'Uncle Bert, with his drooping moustache and old tweed jackets, often came on holiday with us,' immediately conjures up a picture that they can keep in mind. It may inspire you to add a little more to bring him to life. 'He loved to fish in rock pools with us, and built a little aquarium where we could keep our catches overnight.'

Avoid long lists of names in the story; you can always include a separate 'cast list' at the beginning or end. This is a common fault, even in certain highly regarded novels that bring in too many characters too quickly and end up driving the reader crazy! You find yourself flicking back through the pages, scanning for a mention of Emily who has just reappeared on the page. Was she the elderly seamstress, or possibly the vivacious young cousin? After a short while, you cease to care. So in your life story, do better than some of the great writers: have a 'duty of care' to your readers, and make sure they can follow your developing narrative by giving context to your characters. If you reintroduce people into the story, after an absence in the narrative, it's often a good idea to put in 'reminders' as to who they are. You will have no problem remembering, but your readers might.

Context

Creating context in your life story is about setting the scene, and filling in the background to your story. This is partly out of need, in order to explain what you're writing about, but also because you can add interest by rounding out the context. For instance, if you are writing about how you were working in Hong Kong during the handover to China, you will need to explain briefly that it had been in British hands, but that there was an agreement to transfer sovereignty back to China on 1 July 1997. Not everyone, especially younger generations, will know how Hong Kong changed rulership and there are plenty of us who have already forgotten exactly when it was.

Then, once you've filled in the essential details, you have the option to give more background information if you wish. In this case, you might want to describe the life and culture of Hong Kong, or to explain the lead-up to the handover, by talking about how Britain had acquired the territory in the nineteenth century on a ninety-nine-year lease. Don't be tempted to give a whole history lesson though. A few well-chosen facts are better than pages of explanation.

The extent to which you expand any context in your story depends on your own circumstances. If, for instance, Hong Kong was very important in your own life, or if you were brought up there, you will probably want to set the scene in more detail. But if you only worked there for a year, then basic information will be enough, and you can always enliven it by recounting your own anecdotes about your time in the colony.

Filling in too much context could also mean that you will exhaust yourself, and begin to doubt that you can ever finish the story. Keeping context concise and making sure that information is trimmed to the contours of your story will help to keep the momentum going. Remember that you can always come back later and add in a little more, and you can also take the opportunity to put in extra pages of information in an appendix.

If you consult other sources, such as guidebooks, history books or even Internet sites, be careful on copyright issues when it comes to including extracts from these, or using photocopies of their pages. Even depositing your life story with a local-history archive could, in theory, infringe copyright, if you've quoted from other sources. So unless you are absolutely sure that the material is copyright-free, or that only your close friends and family will see your life story, be sure to write everything in your own words.

Here are the main types of context that you will need to fill in when writing your story.

HISTORICAL CONTEXT

As your story unfolds, describe something about the times you have lived through, with details of the period. We are all, whether we like it or not, walking history. Little details of domestic life – how the streets looked, the games you played at school – really enhance the narrative, and can be fascinating for readers born in a different era. You may also need to explain certain aspects of the period. For example, if you grew up in the 1950s, you might write about your family's first television set and what a thrill it was to watch, but to make sense of this for younger readers, you will also need to state that owning a TV was both a novelty and a luxury at the time. You could also fill in a few more details, such as the tiny screens, test cards and fuzzy black-and-white pictures.

Here is a writing exercise which blends personal experience with the history of the times. I've suggested two different approaches, one looking at an innovation in the domestic sphere, and the other connecting to a major event on the world stage. Trying out both gives a sense of how both small and large-scale changes impact on our lives, and these two pieces of writing may well be suitable for inclusion in your complete life story narrative.

Exercise: new horizons

1. Think of an incident or occasion when something completely new from the period was introduced into your childhood home. It could be the first television that your family owned, an automatic washing machine or even a make of instant pudding. Allow yourself a few minutes to recall this. You can make notes, or use the 'bubble' exercise on p. 12 if you like to jot down your impressions. What did this new thing look like, taste like or sound like? Why was it special and different? Who was there? What did you or your parents do with it? Next, write a paragraph or two about the experience. Try to include any atmosphere that it created, any sensations associated with it that you recall.

You will probably find that even in such apparently trivial events, stories are embedded, and a whole context of your family, and the way you lived, unfolds. Nothing that you write about in this way will be boring, if you bring in the human element.

2. You may also have lived through significant historical events, such as a war or national crisis, and by recording your memories of these you can make a valuable contribution to social history as well as leaving a narrative for those close to you. Once again, though, keep your main objective in mind; make *your* life history the prominent thread, rather than too long a discourse on history itself. But even in a very personal narrative, do consider weaving in mentions of world events, especially if you have built these into your chronology, as suggested in Chapter Two (see pp. 24–25).

Choose one such event, and write about the way in which it unfolded, and how it affected you. Try and recall the immediate details of your experience, in much the same way as we worked on describing an early memory (see pp. 45–47). Then say, if relevant, how it changed your life in general. Was your attitude different afterwards? Did it influence your lifestyle? Were there direct repercussions in your own family? The nature of the event will of course dictate the kind of effects that you describe, which could be as dramatic as losing your home in a World War II air raid, or learning thrifty housekeeping as a result of food shortages during the 1973 Oil Crisis.

Here is my own account of the death of President Kennedy:

> The day President Kennedy was assassinated, on 22 November 1963, I was fourteen years old. That evening, I was sitting at home on my own, feeling very grown up to be in charge of the house while my parents played bridge next door. When the newsflash came through on TV, interrupting whatever quiz or comedy programme was on at the time, I ran straight out of the house, using the gap in the fence as a shortcut, to bang on the neighbours' door. I felt very important, bringing the news, and I could see the intense impact it had on my parents. One day later that week, a group of us from school walked miles on our own initiative to sign the Book of Condolence in Birmingham. It was a strange, sad occasion; we were too young to feel it keenly, but old enough to sense the world was changing around us, and that our growing up might take a different course now.

Some books on writing life stories contain lists of prompts to stimulate reminiscence, which can be very useful for jogging the memory. There are also books on recent history which set out the life and times of the twentieth century, decade by decade, and these too are marvellous reminders of what happened when. (See Resources, pp 193–195, for some recommended books.)

Here are a few suggestions to get you started on framing up your memories from a particular era. Although childhood is the most historical era of your life, and it's great fun recalling memories of this time, don't forget that you have undoubtedly lived through some very interesting times in your adult life, and these too can play a part in your story.

Questions from childhood
- What news do you remember hearing on the radio, or seeing on television, when you were very young?
- How did your mother do her washing?
- Did you have deliveries to the house – for instance of coal or groceries?
- What kind of sweets did you buy with your pocket money?
- How did you usually travel around? What were the buses and cars like?
- Do you remember any significant national celebrations – e.g. the end of the war, the Queen's coronation?

Questions from adult life
These will depend on your age, but if some of these periods don't apply, it's easy to invent others for a different era along the same lines:

- Were you a part of the swinging Sixties, and what did they mean to you?
- Where were you when President Kennedy or Princess Diana died?
- Have you lived through a period of strikes or social unrest that affected your life?
- What kind of décor did you choose when you moved into your own home?
- What kind of outfits did you wear as a young adult going out to celebrate?

GEOGRAPHICAL CONTEXT
Include location details for any places which are prominent in your story, either where you may have lived, or connected to key events. As with historical detail, the art is to put in a little description without weighing the narrative down. Here are a few examples, each one contained within a single sentence:

- 'Bath was a smoke-blackened, sleepy town in the early 1960s.'
- 'We lived in a part of Kent which was full of cherry orchards,

and it was still common to see horse-drawn gypsy caravans travelling the roads to help with the fruit picking.'

- 'Birmingham was undergoing a revolution; back-to-back houses were being demolished, high-rise buildings were springing up and the new concrete Bull Ring shopping centre was considered to be the ultimate in modernity.'

Once again, be sure to include any essential facts. Your Australian grandchildren may not have a clue that Bournemouth is a seaside town, unless you tell them!

FAMILY CONTEXT

We've already covered the important points in the last chapter about what to include in terms of your family, so this is just a reminder to set down at least the basic details of your immediate family (siblings and parents), and preferably some information about aunts, uncles and grandparents too. If possible, say a little about each one, or perhaps just highlight some of the more interesting relatives if there are too many to include. Remember that your family story is interlinked with your own individual story, and in order for people to understand your story, they will need to know something of your family as well. Providing a family tree or a cast list in the front or back of your narrative will make it easier for your readers to identify family members, and will save you a lot of work doing this in the body of the life story.

Events and incidents

To bring your story alive, you need to put in a selection of significant events and occurrences. Some may be important life events (new job, death of a parent, marriage or emigration, for instance) and some may be personal events which meant a lot to you, even if they were brief or insignificant to others (winning a race at Sports Day, losing your favourite toy as a child or falling out with a friend).

As a rule of thumb, do:

- Mention all the major events or occurrences which either happened to you or which affected you strongly in the time span that you're covering, even if you don't describe them all in detail.
- Write fuller accounts of a selection of events to bring them vividly to life.

In case this sounds obvious, consider the following narrative. It is fictitious, but typical of the way in which life stories are all too often written. Let's say that it's by Ken, a man in his fifties, who is keen to set down an account of his life, but is a little shy about doing so.

> I took my A Levels, left school and got a job in the local town-planning office. Then I moved to Guildford where I met my wife, and began working for an undertaker's firm. This didn't suit me, so after our first child was born, we moved again to Woking and I retrained as an accountant and found a position in a company specialising in handling finances for show-business personalities.

What opportunities have been lost there! Ken didn't want to bore anybody, but in his modesty, he has actually drained the narrative of interest. These are some of the questions that he could have answered, spinning vivid accounts around them.

- What was your first day at work like as a school leaver?
- How did you meet your wife?
- What kind of things did you have to do at the undertaker's?
- Say more about your first child, and what it was like having a baby in the family?
- What was the accountancy training like?
- Have you got any stories about your show-biz clients?

Although you obviously can't include every single event in your life, don't leave your readers frustrated. It needn't take long to sketch out an incident, or slip in an anecdote. Try the following exercise:

Exercise: the first day

Pick a 'first-day 'experience from your adult life – your first day at work, as a new parent, arriving abroad for the first time or whatever it might be. Write a paragraph about this, and the way it happened, including any funny or serious moments. Include some detail about the place or people involved to help bring it all to life.

Now do the exercise again, but this time change from the past tense to the present, re-writing it the way you wish from this perspective. Write about it as if it were happening right now. For example, instead of saying, 'I was late on my very first day at work,' you are going to say, 'I am late for work.' Perhaps this will stimulate you to say much more? You may find that you are inspired to relate it differently:

> It's ten past nine, and I'm late for work on my very first day! I burst through the door, puffing and offering excuses about the bus that didn't turn up. My new boss raises one eyebrow and goes back to his pile of paperwork. I can see that I'm going to have to try harder to impress anyone around here.

So, by using the present tense, you can create a much more exciting, immediate impact that will grip your readers, and probably you, too, as you relive the moment. Writing in the present tense has become a popular device in novels and life writing; it's not suitable for every occasion, and can look artificial or overdone if it's not judged carefully. But practising in this way can be a brilliant means of opening up your memory and sharpening up your narrative powers. You may find that there are points in your life story where it works really well to switch to the present tense, perhaps to open a new section, or to highlight a significant event.

After you have completed these two ways of expressing the story, put the accounts to one side for a day or so. Then read them again, and rewrite the experience once more. This time, you're going to revert to using the past tense, but including the new details and insights from the present-tense account; see if you can make your account in the past tense more vivid this way.

Summaries

You will probably need to condense certain phases of your life, if you are to cover the whole of your life in one narrative. There is no single approach to selecting which periods to summarise. It could be the ones you are less interested in at the moment, or those which you can't remember too well. It's also possible that there are times in your life which are painful to recall, and you are reluctant to write about them at all. In this particular case, I do suggest that you take the opportunity to mull them over, and see if you can, in fact, find a way of writing about them, if not now, then perhaps later. There is often hidden treasure to be found in our darkest moments; the alchemists say the seeds of gold are present in the blackest material.

In general, however, resorting to summaries in a life story is inevitable, although the reader need not even be aware that you are switching from one pace of narrative to another if you handle it smoothly. Think of a way to summarise the time in question. Was it happy or sad, broadly speaking? Where were you, and with whom? What kind of a life did you have at the time? Take this imaginary example, for instance:

> Those were happy years, when we were settled into family life and we watched the children growing from sweet toddlers into wilful teenagers. Although we had our ups and downs like any family, we enjoyed the process, working in what spare time we had to renovate the old farmhouse we'd bought, and introducing the children to the pleasures of country life – pony riding, picking blackberries, and we even persuaded them to help dig the garden to grow potatoes! I remember taking them out in the morning to feel under the warm breasts of the hens, still sitting on their nests, for brown eggs, perfect for tea-time bread and butter soldiers, and on early summer evenings, we'd all walk over the fields to visit the little pond where tadpoles were turning into frogs.

The reader won't feel cheated by such a narrative because it still has:

- A sense of continuity – there are no awkward gaps, or hints that something has been missed out.
- The context in terms of where the family was living.
- Indications of who was in the family and the stages they were going through (assuming that the children's and spouse's names have been mentioned already).
- Some more detailed descriptions, to create pictures for the reader, in this case about the hens and the tadpoles.

Writing summaries is also a good way of creating continuity in the first draft of your story, if you're not yet sure which parts you want to fill out more. So in general, complete the whole narrative without gaps, but use summaries where you need to. Then you can see how the whole life story pans out, and how long it is in total; if you have the time and desire to do so, you can choose to extend one or more of the phases that you've summarised.

Questions

Reflective questions in your story will help to give it real depth and meaning. These are questions which you can pose about the course your life has taken, the meaning of events, about decisions made and the threads followed. Like other components of the life story, they need to be kept in proportion, and should not swamp the main thrust of the narrative, but, judiciously used, they add an extra dimension to enrich your story.

They may also be beneficial in your own process of reconciling yourself to life events, or perhaps in healing wounds that these have caused. They can bring new wisdom by shedding light on old issues; the spiritual content of a life story, for example, is an aspect which is often overlooked, perhaps because it's difficult to incorporate, or because people are reluctant to open up their hearts and expose their core beliefs in this way. The technique of posing and responding to gentle questions in your life story can provide a means of expressing your faith and your values, and perhaps a way of touching on religious experiences that you have had. And this can also apply to the confirmed atheist or open-minded agnostic, who may also have wrestled with their views, and have interesting points to express, or experiences to recount.

This is a prelude to the final two chapters of the book, in which you'll investigate the choices made in your life, the turning points and the whole journey that you've taken, and which should help you to frame up the questions that you want to pose. You may then decide to address them openly in your life story or you can just keep them in mind as you create your narrative, and allow relevant thoughts to emerge wherever appropriate. Exploration is often the key; the best questions are those which stimulate us and lead us to think more deeply, not necessarily producing any definite conclusions.

The questions can be general or specific; they can be about your life as a whole, your experiences, the world around you, or they can be philosophical or spiritual. You might want to think up some questions before you start your story, but you could also allow others to emerge as you write. Here are some examples:

- Did I make the right decision to train as a nurse?
- How did our family deal with my father's early death?
- If I had taken that job in Africa, how might it have altered my life?
- Have my beliefs and values changed over the years?
- Have I found my real task in life?
- What have I passed on to my children?

A clear beginning and end

Creating a strong beginning and a positive end is an essential part of good writing, and while a life story does not need to be highly charged like a work of fiction, it still needs to start by focusing the reader's interest, and to round off well at the end.

THE BEGINNING

This part is not so difficult in a life story if you follow one of the usual devices, such as starting with your first memory or by introducing yourself with your name and when and where you were born. Or, as we saw on page 133, opening with the present time can also work well.

Here are a few more tips to help you:

- Keep the pace moving for at least a few paragraphs after the opening, before beginning any longer descriptions or explanations. This will give your readers the sense that the story is going somewhere.
- Move with reasonable speed through the first few years of your story too, rather than lingering too long on a description of your babyhood or very early experiences, so that the reader can sense that you are already mapping out a route for the narrative.
- Introduce only a few characters in the opening pages, so as not to overburden the memory of the reader or dull their appetite to continue.
- Include a few events or incidents rather than just background information, in order to show that this really is a narrative, not just a description.

THE END

The end is less easy, because the story is not over yet! This brings us back to making a decision about whether you want to cover your whole life in the narrative, or just certain periods, and it's one that's best resolved before you begin writing, so that you can work towards it and know where the narrative is leading.

End on a positive note if you can; this is not to say that you should hide any difficult circumstances or pretend that everything is lovely if it plainly isn't, but it is worth trying not to be overly negative at the conclusion of your story. A life story is, after all, a life-affirming endeavour; you clearly value it enough to want to write about it, and you have asked others to join you on that journey, in reading it. They will empathise with you, and have a certain kind of faith in you as a person, so if you remain true to yourself, and keep faith with your own worth, your readers will be with you all the way. If, however, you are tempted to end on a bitter or dismissive note, they are likely to feel betrayed and to wish they hadn't engaged with your story earlier. Try to keep this in mind, and to tackle any tragedies, unhappiness or misfortune earlier in the narrative.

Writing Guidelines

So we've looked at the seven building blocks of the story, and now we come to the writing process itself. The emphasis in this book is on telling the story in an authentic way, and producing the highest standard of written English is not the main aim. Indeed, it's often better *not* to be too self-conscious about the finer points of style and grammar when writing a life story. The truth of the narrative and the individual voice in which you tell it are far more important. However, most people want to do their best within that brief, and some guidelines to adding interest to your writing and enhancing the end result can be helpful. The following six techniques are designed with this in mind:

1. Gather your notes and ideas and expand your material first.
2. Look for sources of inspiration in writing beyond the life story framework.
3. Write in full, then select down and edit.
4. Choose material for appendices, notes or extra sections.
5. Use 'close-up' and 'long shot' for variety.
6. Let dialogue bring your narrative to life.

1. Expand your material first

Gather plenty of ideas together, and perhaps write some trial passages for your life story before you begin to fit it all into a tight framework. Allow some preliminary time for mulling over your project, and for collecting material and noting down ideas. Good writing needs to 'breathe', and should not be forced on to the page too quickly. Of course, you may have time constraints, and need to get the project under way, so endless procrastination isn't recommended either. But do allow yourself at least a few weeks to explore your ideas, if you can. It's often quicker in the long run, rather than starting a narrative only to realise after a spell of hard work that it's not going in the right direction.

THE NOTEBOOK

Take a notebook or voice recorder around with you wherever you go. Once you begin to think about your life story, you'll probably find that ideas and recollections pop up at all sorts of inconvenient moments. Jot them down or make a voice memo; often a few key words will do as a reminder for later.

THE CREATIVE PROCESS

The process of writing is a creative one, and for 'creative', also read 'mysterious'. Much of it happens out of sight, away from your conscious thought process. It's extraordinary how an idea can seemingly pop up out of nowhere, or how that mass of detail you were trying to get into shape yesterday appeared in crystalline clarity this morning.

In writing, it's important to trust this process. So allow time for exploration, expansion and the gathering of thoughts and memories. Then, if you are concerned that you now have too much material on hand, take a step back from it. Turn your attention elsewhere for a few hours, days or weeks, and when you return to it, you are far more likely to see how to select and order what you have.

2. Inspiration beyond the life story

Since my interest in life stories began, I've read a lot more autobiographies, memoirs and travel writing. These have given me useful insights into the techniques of good 'life writing', as the genre is known – into ways of tackling emotional issues, writing accounts that are both funny and moving, bringing events vividly to life and also courageously exploring the deeper questions of the story.

There are also many collections of oral history accounts available which can be fascinating too, such as the ongoing American *Story Corps* project and the early British Mass Observation experiment, for which people were encouraged to keep diaries of their everyday lives. Historically, Henry Mayhew's interviews with the 'London Poor' in the nineteenth century, where he allowed individuals such as a street sweeper, a flower girl and a sewer man to recount their own stories, are a revelation. In a different vein, *Aubrey's Brief Lives* from an earlier period includes touching and personal details of prominent figures of the day, many of them gathered from the memories of their friends and servants.

All of these types of life writing can be a source of interest and practical tips for anyone who is writing their life story. You will not have to look far to find them: your own bookshelves, the local library, the Internet (Darwin's account of his travels are freely available online, for instance) and, of course, bookshops. There is a selection of recommended reading in Resources (see p. 191), but you should have no trouble finding plenty yourself and choosing according to your own interests.

When it comes to using these resources, it's worth keeping the following in mind:

- Remember that you are going to write your life story in *your* way, using your own voice. Don't try to emulate any of the authors that you read; it can come across as phoney and may stifle your own style.
- If you are interested in analysing the skills of other writers more closely, you could turn to manuals for creative writing students (see Resources, pp. 192–193).
- Keep your main objective in mind, which is to write your life story. Should you decide to study different forms of writing (fiction, poetry, etc.), this may work best as a separate project, or something you come back to when you've finished your narrative, otherwise it could be hard to get your story under way.

3. Write, then edit

I've suggested gathering together more ideas and material than you can use, and the same principle applies to the writing itself. Allow your writing to flow and expand on the page before you tidy it up too much. But do follow up by editing it. It's a good idea in the first instance to be expressive, to take risks and to write too many words, but then the work needs to be carefully honed. I once knew a famous opera star who wrote his memoirs for publication, but then refused to allow his editor to make any changes, thinking that his inspiration would be muddied if it was tampered with in any way. When I read the book, I found it both rambling and self-indulgent; it would certainly have benefited from some expert editing and the result was that it didn't stay in print for long.

THE EDITING PROCESS

All writers need a degree of objectivity in writing, whether that's provided by an outside editor, or by themselves. The process varies from person to person, but a typical approach would be to give your writing reasonably free rein in your first draft, before coming back to it with a fresh eye. Then, as well as polishing the style, be prepared to cut any superfluous words or phrases; you'll often find that your writing becomes much more striking once you've done this.

Editing can be hard graft, often much more than the original outpouring of words. You may need to go through your text a couple of times at least before it's in good shape. I usually do a fairly loose first edit, without fretting about every last word. I know that later on I may want to make insertions or juggle the text around some more, so I simply get it into 'good enough' shape, before moving on to the next section. Then, when the project is complete, I go through it with an eagle eye, checking both the little details and the flow and structure of the entire narrative.

Tip:
Work hard at your editing, harder even than at your writing.

FORMATTING AND CHECKING: AIM FOR CLARITY AND CONSISTENCY

You may have noticed as you read through this book that the text is divided into various headings and subheadings, each formatted in a specific way. It's useful to adopt a similar approach in your life story, whereby you indicate different types of breaks, headings or sections, using bold print, italics, capitals and so on. So, for example, use one style to indicate a new chapter, another for sections within that and yet another for any subheadings within each section. If you are writing by hand, you may not have as many options at your disposal, but underlining and/or use of capitals is a straightforward way to indicate breaks and sections. You're unlikely to need as many styles as there are in this book, but it will help you to organise your material in this way and the reader to follow your train of thought. This can easily be done at the editing stage. Or, if you've already imposed a system, now is the time to check that your formatting styles are consistent and that they work as signposts in the text.

Using a computer also gives you the benefit of spelling and grammar checking tools, which can be a real boon in pointing out places where you have misplaced an apostrophe or repeated a word without realising it. I was convinced that 'misspelt' should have only one 's' until my computer corrected me! Make sure that your language preferences are set correctly – it can be highly irritating to find that your computer insists on American spelling if you're in Britain, and vice versa. If you are writing by hand you might need the input of a kind friend just to check for dodgy spelling and grammar. However, whether you are working with a computer or by hand, do take any suggestions with a pinch of salt, and make your own decisions; language is an ever-changing thing, and rules that used to be absolute, like never using a split infinitive, are now more flexible.

'SLAUGHTER YOUR DARLINGS'

In writing, there is an expression, 'Slaughter your darlings'. It sounds painful – I resisted the notion when I first heard it, but, over the years, I have found it to be one of the most useful maxims around. But what does it mean exactly? Well, we all have our pet ideas, polished phrases that we can't wait to trot out or, perhaps, a pontification on the state of the universe that we would like to pass on to our readers for their edification. Giveaway signs are statements like, 'I have always found that . . .', 'I have come to the conclusion that . . .', 'It's my belief that . . .' Put them down in writing if you must, but then, if you are honest, you will probably find that they stick out like a sore thumb. So kill them off at birth. They *may* be the prelude to wonderful words of wisdom, but then again, they may not. And rather than enlivening a narrative, they may deaden it, or lead you and the reader off on an irrelevant digression. So do please 'slaughter your darlings'!

REPETITIONS AND RHYTHMS

Look out too, for repetitions. We all repeat words without realising it. Here is a simple example:

> I often used to see my relatives at Christmas, and among the relatives that I have, Cousin George was the funniest. He used to put on a kilt and dance around the Christmas tree doing the Highland Fling. Other relatives in the room used to fall about laughing, and try to copy him . . .

Spot the multiple use of the word relatives! English is a brilliant language for synonyms, alternative words and phrases with the same meaning, so don't be afraid to seek them out when you need them.

Now let's try it this way:

> I often used to see my relatives at Christmas, and Cousin George was the funniest among them. He used to put on a kilt and dance around the Christmas tree doing the Highland Fling. Other members of the family who were there would fall about laughing, and try to copy him . . .

Here, I have changed one use of the word 'relatives' to 'members of the family' and have removed another entirely, substituting 'them' instead, and changing the word order to balance up the sentence.

I've also changed the wording slightly in the final sentence because it sounded better once I had made the alterations. When you make changes in your writing, test out the rhythm of the edited sentence to see if it still works.

You may notice some repetitions as you write, and you can change these on the spot, whereas others will only catch your eye later on when you edit. I can guarantee that you'll wonder how on earth you missed some of them first time round.

Tip:

Try reading your work out loud sometimes to check for rhythm and to listen for repetition.

4. Appendices, notes and extra sections

The appendix has been mentioned before (see p. 100), but deserves a mention here as well, as a tool in your writing repertoire. If you find yourself struggling with a weighty chunk of information, consider turning it into an appendix. Here are some suggestions for material that might be consigned to the end of the life story (those marked with an asterisk could also appear at the front of the narrative):

- historical notes
- background information on a geographical place
- a list of the characters in your story*
- brief sketches of the lives of some of the people mentioned in the story
- your chronology or timeline*
- description of a job or profession that features in the narrative
- a family tree*
- letters that are relevant to your story
- extracts from newspapers or journals connected with the events you are describing.

The term 'appendix' can sound heavy and forbidding, so you may choose to use 'endnotes' instead or simply list the various entries individually – 'Timeline, Family Tree and Selected Letters', for instance.

You can write up entries for an appendix as you go along, or simply jot down ideas now, then work on them after you have finished the main narrative.

5. Close-ups and long shot

The use of close-up and long shot (see also pp. 67–68) in a narrative can help you to create an interesting texture that keeps the reader engaged. A good film or TV programme does not usually hold the picture continually at the same distance from the action; cameras are positioned both for close-up and long-shot filming, which will give the viewer a change of perspective and in doing so, convey different information about the subject.

A simple way of using this technique in your life story is to give a long shot of a particular theme, then a close-up to recount a specific event that occurred in connection with it. So, for instance, an account of your time at secondary school might start with a general description – a long shot – of the teachers, lessons and classrooms, then it could include a close-up, homing in on the day you played truant and ran off to town with a couple of your friends.

Here's another short, fictitious example. (Perhaps it could even be an extension of the photo described on p. 56 of two little children on a beach.)

> We used to go to the beach often in the summer months, taking a picnic which my mother guarded until we'd had our swim and perhaps made a few sandcastles. The beach was very long, with no cliffs or bushes, just a rather bleak expanse of sea and sand. Mostly, we enjoyed these expeditions though.
>
> One day, however, when I was paddling in the sea, I saw what I thought was a horrible monster coming towards me. I remember how hard it was to get away. The little pink and

green ruched bathing costume I was wearing was heavy with water and my toes seemed to get sucked deeper and deeper into the sand as I tried to run back on to the beach. It was a jellyfish, swimming ever closer to me. I screamed and screamed. My brother, who usually mocked my fears, realised there was something seriously wrong and raced towards me, snatching me up just in time as the jellyfish brushed against my legs. I don't know whether it would have stung me or not, but I'm glad I didn't have to find out. From that time on, I began to look on my brother more as a protector, and less as an adversary.

There is contrast between these two shots, both in terms of time and description; in other words, the long shot is both a broad view of the landscape and of the years during which the narrator visited that beach. The close-up focuses on a few minutes in time, and on a very small area of space: it is a picture of one small girl in the water and a boy running to join her. Notice too, that the passage is rounded off with a reflective comment, a good way to explain why the incident was important, and to lead the way back to the next development or long shot in the story.

You may well find that you already include elements of close-up and long shot in your writing to some degree. Even so, it's useful to identify these techniques, since having a conscious understanding of how they work can help us to employ them in a more skilful and consistent way. Using close-up and long shot mindfully can really help to shape the contours of your account.

6. Dialogue

There is a tendency to recount everything in a life story without using dialogue or direct speech. In a very short life story, such as the blueprint version we worked on earlier (see pp. 62–88), you may find it tricky to include dialogue, but in a longer version, it's an excellent way of bringing events alive.

What do you feel when you read the following?

I was summoned to the boss's office. He told me that the company was going through a lean period and that they were going to make me redundant. I wondered what I was going to do, with the mortgage to pay and a family to feed.

That's a perfectly acceptable piece of narrative. But it isn't riveting; it doesn't give you a sense of the action happening before your eyes. So how about changing some of it into dialogue? This will generate extra detail, which will also help to enliven the account:

It was a frosty day in February. I was just settling down to my morning's work in the office, when the boss's secretary approached me.

'Mr Forbes wants to see you straight away.'

A summons from the boss was rare, and I entered his office apprehensively.

Forbes was a large man, with dishevelled hair, who always had a drip on the end of his nose in cold weather. He hummed and hawed for a few minutes, asking questions about my family while I shifted my position restlessly.

He finally got round to it. 'Well, Andrew, I'm very sorry to have to tell you that the company is struggling to get enough orders at the moment. We're going to have to let one or two members of staff go, and you, I'm afraid, are one of them.'

I could hardly speak. 'But – what about the project I'm working on?'

'That will be passed on to the others in your team. We're having to reduce the senior staff, you see. Economics, I'm afraid. Rules the world, doesn't it?'

'I've been with the company for twenty-three years now. I have a mortgage, a growing family. . .'

He waved it away. 'I know, I know. It's tough. We'll give you all the settlements you're entitled to of course. And I'm sure you won't have trouble finding a job elsewhere.'

Oh wouldn't I? He was washing his hands of me, I could see that. And it's just as well I didn't know then what I know now –

that it would take me five years, a marriage break-up, and near
bankruptcy before I got back on my feet again.

A worry which commonly arises on switching to dialogue is that often
you can't remember the exact words that were said at the time. But, in
my view, as long as you remain faithful to the spirit of the original incident, it doesn't matter. If you look at published autobiographies, for
instance, you'll see that the authors frequently use direct speech. Are
their memories any better than yours? Almost certainly not. They have
simply reconstructed dialogue in a way that works within the narrative.

The secret is to write the dialogue in a lively manner, following
the gist of what you remember, but not aiming to use the precise
words of the original speech. Ideally, it should be in keeping with the
characters and their responses. This does not mean making up a better
story, or putting in the things you wish you'd said at the time. It's a
way of bringing the conversation back to life in the best way you can,
using a literary device which will help you to recreate the memory
more vividly for yourself and your readers.

Seven Components, Six Techniques

We've now covered the seven key components or building blocks for
constructing your life story, and the six techniques that will help you
to write it. It's up to you how much use you make of these guidelines,
and how far you would like to raise your writing standards, as opposed
to simply endeavouring to commit the story to paper while you have
the time and inclination. Whatever your outlook, I recommend that
you keep this chapter to hand as a reference point when planning and
writing your story. Further your creativity by training the robot,
unleashing the dragon, and letting them loose together in the magical pool of your story!

CHAPTER SEVEN

The Meaning of Life

We have covered all the basic techniques of life story writing now, and the final two chapters are designed to help you to go deeper into your experience, and to see the pattern and shape of your life. Following the suggestions and exercises in them will generate valuable ideas and pieces of writing that you can include directly in the narrative if you wish, or which can serve as a general influence in your writing. Whichever way you choose to use the insights gained from these chapters, they will help to infuse your story with the truth at the heart of your being, the essential 'you', which your readers want to discover.

'The meaning of life' is a well-used phrase, so much so that it can even be considered something of a joke. Nevertheless, the question 'What is the meaning of life?' is still one of the most serious you can pose. This view is shared by the free Internet encyclopaedia, Wikipedia, which solemnly declares:

> The meaning of life constitutes a philosophical question concerning the purpose and significance of human existence. The concept can be expressed through a variety of related questions, such as *Why are we here? What's life all about?* and *What is the meaning of it all?*

It then declares, plaintively:

This article is in need of attention from an expert on the subject. Please help recruit one or improve this article yourself.

So who or what constitutes an expert on the meaning of life? Can you or I be counted as experts in this respect, and add our store of wisdom to the question if we wish? I believe we can. Philosophers and spiritual teachers have certainly given us valuable insights into the nature of life, but, ultimately, each of us has to recognise its meaning for ourselves. We are all experts in our own way, if we take the trouble to try and understand what life means and has meant to us.

In this chapter, ways of tapping into this level of meaning are suggested, which can yield rich material for your life story. They may give you insights into the most significant aspects and events of your life; they may also arouse strong emotions, as well as being enjoyable and illuminating.

Tackling these exercises requires honesty, and although you may not emerge with a perfect answer to the question, 'What is the meaning of life?' you stand to gain greatly in discovering what has made *your* life meaningful to *you*.

Writing About Your Treasured Possessions

Describing the most treasured objects in your possession is a practical and immediate way of identifying this level of meaning in your life. In the following exercise, you'll choose up to three items which represent something special. In Chapter Five, we worked on objects associated with your family or ancestors (see pp. 116–118). Here, they should be ones which have strong personal associations to you as an individual. They may connect with the family, but also be a part of your own experience. Such an object could symbolise a certain moment or period in your life or a significant event in it. (Glance ahead to the list at the end of this section, on pp. 153–154, if you are unsure as to what kind of thing to choose.)

Exercise: 'Things I will never get rid of'

Pick three treasured objects in your possession. If you have more than three to choose from, pick ones from different times in your life, or those which have very different meanings for you. If, on the other hand, you're finding it difficult to find suitable objects, take a walk around your home or rummage in your drawers to jog your memory. It's surprising how many small items you may overlook on a day-to-day basis, which actually hold the key to past experience.

Next, fetch the objects from where they are stored or displayed, or go to each of them if they cannot be moved. Look at each one in turn: feel it or handle it as appropriate. Allow your sense of touch to tell you more about it, as well as your eyes. Does it have a particular smell, too? Or perhaps there is a sound associated with it? Allow any memories, feelings or thoughts to arise. Give yourself a few minutes to experience the object, then jot down your impressions in note form.

Follow this by writing a paragraph or two about each object. Keep the writing succinct, and as well as telling the story of the object, say what it means to you.

This is a simple exercise, but one which can evoke profound feelings. Several times, it has moved students to tears in the summer school life story class, so be prepared for it to touch these deeper levels in you.

Below are extracts from three stories written by students in the life story class, around objects with international connections. The first was written by Rose who was born in England, but has lived most of her adult life in Switzerland, formerly working for the Swiss national airline. She wrote:

My most treasured objects are my two passports (one Swiss and one British) and my SwissAir identity card. These are the key to the door of the world. My first trip abroad was when I was twelve. My parents took us to Paris on a coach trip. It was so exciting to cross the border – indeed even today after so much travel, I find crossing frontiers thrilling. When we arrived in

France after the Channel crossings, I wrote down everything we did – even at that time I just had to write or 'die'. I collected everything: every ticket, every scrap of paper and of course I took photos with my Brownie Box Camera. It was all wildly interesting.

Rose was not alone in the class in choosing her passport as one of her most prized possessions, and for many people, they hold a cornucopia of memories, which can be released and written up for the life story. Indeed, this quote was just the beginning, and Rose was inspired to write several more pages about her travels.

Tip:

If your passport holds the key to many interesting experiences that you would like to recount, consider using 'My passport' as the theme for a whole section or chapter in your life story.

Colin brought to class a box which had belonged to his father:

My parents lived for many years in the West Indies and in the Bahamas. My father was a very gregarious person and would talk to anyone in any walk of life, and was always interested in small, harmless practical jokes.

When they were in Jamaica, a particular friend, knowing of his many interests, gave him this small wooden box, made from *lignum vitae*, a West Indies hardwood. Engraved on the lid was: 'To the man who has everything – now something to keep it in.' When you opened the box you discovered it was a solid piece of wood cut in half, and therefore had no interior space.

Looking at the box now always brings back memories of my parents, life in Jamaica and my father's many practical jokes.

We have already heard something of Sophia's story (see p. 106), and how her background crosses different cultures; here she writes about a 'cheerful' mug:

> The mug stands on the dresser in my kitchen now – its clear bright reds, blues and greens taking me back to the white-washed kitchen of my Czech grandparents in Moravia. This one and its companion mugs were always there in the kitchen to welcome me when I went to visit my mother's parents, in the 1930s before the war. They were still there when it was again possible to visit Czechoslovakia in the 1960s and '70s, as chinks began to appear in the Iron Curtain. By this time both my grandparents had died; my aunt, my mother's younger sister now lived on her own in the family house, where nothing had changed since the 1940s.
>
> When she died, many of the objects in the family house were brought over to England by me and my sister to keep alive our memories of our Czech roots. I have always loved Slav designs, and the cheerful bold red flowers and bright green leaves on this mug take me back to my teenage years in the country.

OTHER EXAMPLES OF TREASURED OBJECTS

Every single object that members of the life story class have brought to show has been fascinating and often profoundly moving. Here are some more examples, each with a key to what they represent to their owners – you'll see both how varied they are, and how they encapsulate a gamut of experiences and attendant emotions:

- A display panel of designs and embroidery – this was produced during a happy and creative year's study on a sewing course.
- An army ID card used on a military exercise in France, involving three days' rough travelling undercover to reach a destination 100km away without being discovered.
- A gold muff chain which belonged to one woman's grandmother in Australia – her own mother always wore it,

and one day she decided that it was the right moment to pass it on to her daughter, who treasures it as a symbol of the maternal line.

- A musical instrument – a recorder – which symbolises the important place music has had in this lady's life, and the joy it brings.

- 'Beppo' the monkey, a soft toy – its owner, now over eighty, has had it since she was six. Beppo has travelled with her everywhere, and now wears a miniature rucksack taken from a key ring, and a suit made from a pair of knickers.

- The wedding ring of a widow, a joyful reminder of a long life shared together, tinged with the sorrow of loss now that her husband has passed away.

- A few drops of North Sea oil sealed into a block of glass, signifying the history of pioneering for oil in the North Sea and how closely the enterprise was tied up with this man's career.

- A woman's father's watch (he had died only a month earlier). Its three dials show different world times, and he loved to set them to where his children were living or working abroad.

- A laptop computer; this signifies the owner's long career with computers, and the changes that have taken place in the world since he began work.

- Granny's bed socks, chosen as a memento from her possessions. This grandmother was a very spiritual and interesting person, and her granddaughter (now retired herself) wears these socks daily when practising her meditation and yoga.

- A tiny silver dog given by a young man to his father when the old man was dying, and which has now returned to the son's possession. The son gave it to his father to signify his faithfulness and love, his regret for the bad times he had caused in the past, and as a symbol of taking responsibility for his own life now. The father was holding it when he died.

- Coloured sands in a glass jar from the Grand Canyon, Colorado. For one woman these are the essential memory of a fascinating trip to the US taken with an American friend, a chance to see the States from an insider's point of view.

TIPS FOR WORKING IN GROUPS: EXERCISING TRUST

In a group or class situation, it requires a certain amount of trust for someone to show their special mementos, and to talk about their significance. After all, such items can be associated with the most painful, joyful or profound experiences of a person's life. So if you are using this book to work with others, allow several sessions to pass before introducing the previous exercise, and only do so when you are confident that there is a level of mutual understanding and empathy between the participants.

In a group, this exercise can work even better if it is spoken aloud, as opposed to written. This makes it easier to bring an object's associations to life, and its meaning will be more immediate and vivid. Writing about it straight away in class could stifle the feelings surrounding it, whereas talking about it first is likely to reveal their true depth, to the owner as well as to everyone else. For this approach, participants are asked in advance to bring their chosen objects – one per person will do for a group session – and are given a few minutes to write some notes about what they would like to say. Then the object can be shown or passed around while the owner talks about its meaning and connections. The full account can be written up afterwards, either during the session or at home.

After someone has described their treasured object, it's helpful to invite comments and questions, but criticism would not be appropriate in this sensitive situation.

The Day My Life Changed

One of the beautiful things about reaching this stage of the life story project is that the themes we are now working with are profound but simple. They don't need much in the way of explanation, or technique; it's as though the gear has been prepared for mining, the equipment tested and we can now delve down into the deeper levels of experience and memory to search out the gemstones lying hidden below. Maybe we will even find a few diamonds there and bring them up into the light of day.

'The Day My Life Changed' is an exercise along these lines which I devised from a book of the same name, by Carmel Reilly. It is an inspiring collection of first-hand individual accounts, about moments that changed people's lives for ever. Some of these are dramatic, like an accident, whereas others are subtle, such as a chance remark from a stranger which changed the person's outlook and thus the course of events in their life. Some are tragic – deaths, suicides, diagnoses of terminal illnesses – but others are joyful, such as weddings, triumphs and the launching of new careers. Many are to do with love and friendship, family intimacy, and many, too, have a spiritual dimension. In all of them, there are revelations of lessons and realisations, epiphanies and inspirations, gifts and promises, loss and transcendence. And above all, they show how deeply people reflect upon their lives, and the wisdom that they distil from the changes that happen to them.

I have chosen one to quote here, with the kind permission of the publisher. It was hard to select just one, since there are so many crying out to be shared, but perhaps you will be able to read the original book for yourself (see p. 193 for details). The runners-up were one account of how a prisoner turned his life around by attending a poetry workshop in prison, and another of how a woman finally lost her stage fright by singing at her sister's wedding. But I've opted for Frank's story of how he lost and reclaimed his life, all in a few short minutes:

> I nearly lost my wife and child last year. We had been visiting
> my sister a few miles away, and we were walking down a city

street back to my car. My wife and daughter were walking just ahead of me. Elsa, my daughter is four years old, and we have problems teaching her to be careful around roads. She tends to walk right along the edge of the road, which makes us nervous at the best of times. She is very obstinate. She was walking ahead of my wife.

Suddenly a car screeched around the corner and came careering towards us. I thought maybe it was being chased by another car or something. It all happened very fast. I tried to shout to my wife, and she was looking round at the same time, but right in front of me the car slid across and came quite fast up on to the pavement. It hit my wife Karine with a glancing blow and she fell hard against the pavement and rolled over. She was knocked out, other than that I had no idea how bad it might be. The car rolled right up and ran into the wall, then stopped, with the engine still running.

I couldn't see Elsa at all. I was terrified that she might be under the car. The man got out of the car, on the side away from me, and just started running. I can't believe that even now. It is terrible to not even stop to see what you have done.

I ran around the car and Elsa was lying on the ground, face down the same as Karine. I thought they might both be dead. Someone ran out of the house beside me and said that an ambulance had been called. I ran back to Karine and she was unconscious, with a bit of blood around her mouth and a cut on the side of her head. I could see right away she was breathing, which was something. The woman who had come out of a house knelt down beside her, so I ran back to Elsa.

And amazingly, just as I got there, she was standing up, looking very confused. 'What happened?' she asked. 'Where's Mummy?' It was a complete miracle, but all that had happened was that she had been knocked off her feet and fallen over. Either the car had hit her just as it stopped, or she had been knocked over by the rush of air behind her back. It must have been the closest escape possible, but all she had was a grazed knee. I grabbed her and picked her up and we ran back to Karine. Elsa was still confused and was telling her to wake up.

Then the ambulance came and we all went to the hospital. Karine was unconscious for a couple of hours, and she was quite concussed when she woke up. She was also in a lot of pain because she had cracked a rib. It took about six weeks to heal and she was uncomfortable for that time. But she was alive.

It changed my life because it made me stop and reassess all my priorities. As far as I was concerned, I had seen them die and then they had come back to life. That was how it felt. And now I had them both back I was determined to make sure that I made the best of things. I haven't always been the best father or husband. I can be bad tempered and difficult to be around, and I didn't always do my share around the house. But I've tried to change – I may not be perfect now, but I appreciate what I have and I am trying much harder.

What has made a difference in your life? If you could pick one moment, one event, one day in your life that has changed you for ever, what would it be? Not everyone has experienced a dramatic incident that has overturned their life as they knew it. But everyone, I believe, undergoes a major shift of some kind and at some point – whether of circumstances, of inner attitude or, perhaps, of spiritual knowledge – which puts life on to a new footing. You may well be able to think of more than one such occasion but, for the purposes of this exercise, select the one which you would most like to write about, and which you would be happy to include in your written life story. It doesn't have to be a very unusual event in itself; it's the impact that it had on you which counts, so it could be one of the typical staging posts of life, such as a marriage, a death, the birth of a child or a move of house, for instance.

Choose one such occasion, and ask yourself what changes it brought about, and what difference it made to your life. Then write about it in whatever form you like, as long or as short as you please. This is an exercise that provides you with great storytelling opportunities, making use of suspense and other devices.

Storytelling

Elaine's story of the day that changed her life held our class spellbound as it began with a stirring account of an early-morning ride on the downs with her boyfriend many years ago, galloping through the dewy grass in the dawn. We had no idea where the narrative was going until the couple paused on the summit to admire the rising sun, and the young man suddenly asked her if she would like to emigrate to New Zealand with him. It was a fabulous and completely unexpected resolution to the story, and Elaine concluded it with a brief description of their new life abroad.

Building up suspense might seem to have more of a place in a novel or play, but keeping a sense of drama going gives real edge to a life story too, when events of major importance are being described. There are various ways in which you can help to make your narrative exciting:

- Paint a picture of events for the reader, according to the old writing adage 'show, not tell'.
- Use dialogue, if appropriate.
- Write in the present tense, if it helps to give a sense of immediacy.
- Keep sentences brief, especially when you get to the climax.
- Cut out any unnecessary words, especially adverbs and adjectives.
- Where possible, say what you personally observed and experienced; even if you only have snapshot memories, they are likely to be vivid.
- Keep the reader guessing as to what will happen next; don't preface your story with the outcome.
- Relive the drama as you write it, but go back over it again afterwards in a more detached frame of mind to edit.

A TELEGRAM IN THE BATH

Here is another account from the class, this time by Mary. It was especially valuable when we finally heard it, because Mary had, at first, dug in her heels over this exercise, claiming that nothing had ever happened to change her life! But after further thought, and encouragement from others, she decided to have a go nevertheless, and this was what she came up with:

> My life changed one day when I was seventeen. It was 8 p.m. and I was in the bath. A knock on the door heralded a telegram for me! My father pushed it under the door because I wouldn't let him open it. I got out of the water and dried my hands. The message was from Oxford University: 'We offer you a £40 scholarship to read History.' It was overwhelming.
>
> Weeks ago, I had arrived at school to be chided for being late and rushed upstairs to a little secluded room and told I was sitting the University entrance exam now – no preparation or warning at all. From then, I can't say I was agitated and anxious – in fact, university was right at the back of my mind – so the telegram was a surprise.
>
> When my mother returned, we all got into the car because she decided we must tell the school, and we drove to the Convent and passed on the good news. The next day, my father said, 'I am not sure we can afford to send you,' (my brother was in the second year at university) and I went cold.
>
> But finance was found, and in the autumn, I went to St Anne's College. My life, in a suburb of Birmingham, in a small Convent school, was suddenly entirely different. I was an adult, studying what I wanted to, meeting so many new people, learning to party, how much I could drink and how to understand young men. Terms were only eight weeks long, but exhilarating all the time. When I got home, I would sleep for three days.
>
> Life was never the same; it was lit with colour and hope. The future was mine to control. Not true, of course, but that was how I saw it!

Despite Mary's initial reluctance, the impact of change does come across intensely, and her opening description is a great piece of scene setting. Earlier on in the class, as in this book, we had looked at how to describe memories by recalling the exact details of the scene (see p. 45), and this practice may have helped Mary to create a vivid beginning for the narrative. It is also good storytelling; the effect is to describe a scene which we can follow in our imagination, and to keep us in suspense for a few moments as to the nature of the event.

'The Day My Life Changed' is a chance to write freely and at length if you wish, allowing yourself to experience again the excitement, fear or joy of the moments you are describing. Like everything else in your life story narrative, it can be edited later for length and style, but for now, just immerse yourself in the telling of the tale; if you are reliving it yourself, it will be brought to life for your readers too.

Times of transformation

'The Day My Life Changed' not only gives you a good piece of narrative to slip into your life story, but also points to a moment of transformation in your past, a time when things changed and after which they were never the same again. These moments define who you are as an individual; they are markers along the way, staging posts on your journey through life. If you are to give a meaningful account of your life, one or more of these times of transformation needs to be included in the life story. Otherwise, it could be a worthy but plodding account of 'this happened, then that happened, and then I did such-and-such'. It will serve as a chronicle of your life (like those lists of dates and battles that you had to learn at school), but it won't tell its story.

If I were simply to suggest that you should include a description of how you have changed over the years, you might find it very difficult to write. But by putting the exercise into the context of 'The Day My Life Changed', you gain a handhold, a way of framing up a major point of change, of recalling what led up to it and what followed on from it. It's compelling both as narrative and as an insight into your story.

Once you have completed this exercise, you may find it easier to identify other similar turning points you have experienced, and to understand the kind of transformation that they have generated.

You can then slip them into your story as you go, highlighting some and including a passing reference to others. It may be impossible to include every significant time of change in your life story, but a full description of at least one, and a mention of others, will give your story both colour and meaning.

The Road Not Taken

One day, when I was in my thirties, I was walking through London on my way to a meeting. I was unhappy, unsure about a painful personal decision that I had to take. Just before I reached the street I was heading for, I saw a piece of paper lying on the pavement. I picked it up, unfolded what turned out to be a page from a book, and found a poem printed on it. It was 'The Road Not Taken' by Robert Frost.

In this poem, the poet describes a moment when he is walking through a wood and sees two roads leading in different directions. Which should he choose? Both are beautiful, though one is perhaps less trodden than the other. This is the path he chooses to walk down, and the choice makes 'all the difference' to his life. The poem seemed to speak directly to me, and gave me the confidence to make my decision.

This extraordinary occurrence made a deep impression on me, and the poem has been one of my favourites ever since. I also realised later that it would be a useful concept for life stories too. Which are the roads that you didn't take, the choices you left behind? Like Robert Frost, perhaps you thought you would come back to try them out another day, but maybe, like him, you knew in your heart of hearts that you would never return.

Exercise: which paths have you chosen or left untrodden?

Ask yourself which road you took or passed by on your life's journey. It could be a choice of the college you went to, the person you married, a job you accepted or a place you moved to. It might be something less obvious, such as a resolution to work for fulfilment rather than money. What did you leave behind? How might your life have been if you had taken that other road?

Write a few notes on this, and then a sentence or two for each 'road untaken' that comes to mind. You might write something along these lines, for instance: 'If I had married Steven, rather than Brian, I would have had a more secure life, but a less exciting one. I would have probably become a conventional housewife, rather than going into business with my husband, and entering a new world.'

And what if you feel some regret that you didn't take the other path? This too can be expressed. 'I wish now that I had studied medicine rather than mathematics. I wasn't sure at the time that I was committed enough to spend all those years in training, but the interest in medical matters has never left me, and I would have been happier as a doctor than as a teacher, I think. Volunteering for St John's Ambulance is the closest I've got to it in the life that I chose!'

This is an optional, rather than an essential exercise. Some people do not like looking back to what *might* have happened, and prefer to focus on what actually did take place, and the choices that were made. However, for others, it's intriguing to think about the options which came their way, and how the decisions they made shaped their lives. You cannot always see the point of decision-making itself, as that usually appears in the conscious mind only when the choice has been made at a deeper level. But you can see the implications of that decision, and the untapped potential of the 'road not taken'.

Any work that you do on this theme can be incorporated into your story as part of the 'reflective' commentary that we explored in the last chapter (see pp. 135–136). It may not merit a long section in its own right but by slipping in a few allusions to the options that have come your way in life, you can add value to your story. For children reading a parent's life story, they could even be a revelation. We tend to think that our parents were sure and certain in all the decisions they made, and have no idea of how they might have wrestled with particular choices, and left behind certain possibilities.

Spiritual Dimensions

We live in a time of great change and fluidity in terms of personal faith. A hundred years ago, it would have been, for most people, a simple matter in writing a memoir to state which church or religion they belonged to, or perhaps to take a more radical stance by citing themselves as agnostic or atheist. Nowadays, the picture is far less clear. People may leave the denomination they were brought up in and join another, which could be a major shift from Christian to Buddhist practice, for instance. Others retain nominal links to their childhood faith while pursuing a path of independent enquiry, and others drop all interest in formal religion. There are many permutations of religious background, current faith and personal standpoint, and some of these remain a very private matter, declarations that don't find their way on to hospital forms and public surveys. So there is no single way to include a spiritual dimension in your life story. Added to which, faith itself – as opposed to belief, or doctrine, which can be very specific – is often hard to put into words. The more one tries to do so, the more elusive it becomes.

But is a life story complete if it doesn't contain something of your spiritual beliefs and experience? I would like to suggest two complementary ways of approaching this, the first very simple, and the second with more scope for your personal thoughts.

Naming your religion

At some point in your life story, make a simple statement about the religion, sect or creed you were brought up in (or lack of). Then follow this with an equally simple statement of whether you follow the same or any other practice now. Although this will not get to the heart of your beliefs, it will act as a marker for those reading your life story, especially any descendants who may be following the family story as well. You can then move on to a more expressive description, if you wish, as suggested in the next section.

The pilgrimage

We all make a journey through life, questioning, discovering and witnessing along the way. We encounter conflicting ideas about a loving God, a selfish gene, a transcendent force, a mechanical universe or a world of spirits, and we try to make sense of those concepts, matching them against what we were taught as children, what we read now and the truth of our own experience. This is a pilgrimage, a quest for truth and knowledge, whether you are an atheist, a member of a church or an independent seeker, and writing about this spiritual quest, with its contradictions as well as its moments of illumination, is definitely a part of the story of your life.

Here are some questions to ponder before you begin to write:

- Do you think there is a spiritual world as well as a material one?
- What is your view of good and bad in the universe?
- What do you think about life after death?
- Do you believe in the existence of angels or spirits?
- Could you describe any transcendent or spiritual experiences that have affected your life?
- What particular issues have you wrestled with in relation to your outlook on the world?
- Have you been through any major changes in your faith, beliefs or values?
- Have you met any spiritual teachers or priests who have influenced you significantly?
- Do you worship with others?
- Do you practise meditation or have a personal spiritual practice?
- Are you interested in related subjects, such as astrology, psychic abilities, spiritualism, or magic?

None of these questions is meant to pigeonhole your beliefs too tightly, and I hope they will stimulate further thoughts for you to write about, acting like little magnets, to draw up thoughts, feelings and memories from the depths. Even if some of them seem irrelevant or too simplistic, I recommend that you do consider each one in turn, as you may make new discoveries this way.

When you have worked through the questions, and perhaps made some notes on them, try the following exercise in which you are free to tell the story of the spiritual journey in your own way. You can, of course, keep this completely private, or you can insert it into your life story if you choose. Even if you don't include it, by one of those mysterious processes of osmosis, it is likely to influence your writing thereafter. Putting something down on paper is a magical act; it affects your being and your subsequent creations in subtle ways.

Exercise: the personal quest

Write up to three paragraphs about your spiritual development through life. Write it as if for an unknown reader, one who is sympathetic, wise and non-judgemental. You may find it easiest to use the statements that you framed up in the first section ('Naming your religion', above), modified if need be, and then to move on from there. You could also include any experiences or insights from childhood – it's surprising how profound some of these can be. Mention any particular spiritual path that you have actively followed in adult life, and the people who have influenced you along the way. What point have you reached in your quest now?

THE RULE OF THREE

Writing three paragraphs to explore a view on a particular theme can often be a good way to express your thoughts. In conventional rules of writing too, each paragraph should contain at least three sentences, in order to be a complete entity in its own right. This has its roots in a train of philosophical thought, whereby a debate or argument unfolds thus: thesis, antithesis and synthesis. The first statement (thesis) makes a proposition, the second (antithesis) denies or reacts to it and the third (synthesis) resolves the contradiction or conflict between the other two. Even in a less confrontational form, it makes for a good exposition of a viewpoint or question that you wish to reflect on. In the form of three paragraphs, it works as follows:

1. The opening paragraph makes statements, setting out the facts, argument or the viewpoint.

2. The second paragraph is the 'but' passage, where counter-experiences or opposing arguments and questions come in.

3. The third is the 'resolution', where the outcome, or what you want to say in conclusion, evolves from the opposition found in the first and second paragraphs. Ideally, new thoughts or questions arise from these.

Working Further With the Spiral

I have a small and beautiful fossil of an ammonite that was found by an aunt of mine, which I have had mounted in silver and now wear as a pendant. Not only does it remind me fondly of her, but the spiral-shaped fossil itself intrigues me. It is divided into neat segments, developing from minute ones near the centre to the larger ones on the outer perimeter. I had assumed that a spiral-shaped creature must have lived inside it millions of years ago, and was astonished to learn from a knowledgeable friend that the ammonite never actually inhabited the whole of the spiral, but moved its growing body from one hollow, protective section to the next, into a new and larger chamber as needed and lived only in this final outer segment. The longer it lived, the bigger the spiral grew.

We've already done some work with the spiral in Chapter Four, but let's take another look at it now. A spiral is usually drawn clockwise, in accordance with the movement of the sun, and can be said to represent the sun itself, as well as the growth that circles ever outwards towards infinity. Just as the spiral casing of the ammonite is the actual life story of the creature, so a spiral shape can symbolise the unfolding of a human life. This life grows from its point of origin, spiralling both around and away from it, each coil a little wider than the last, continuing year after year until its close.

There are several different ways to interpret the spiral, which has fascinated human beings for thousands of years. In terms of the life story, there are two predominant meanings that I'd like to suggest here. The first, as we have just seen, is as a symbol of growth and expansion, in the same way that our own story grows and develops over the years. But the second is to do with repeating patterns. Because the growth follows a coiling, circular movement, it also indicates points of repetition where the new spiral pathway mirrors the track of the one below. If you draw a dot on any part of the spiral, for instance, you can put a corresponding dot at the same point on the next line above or below. This symbolises how themes in our lives are constantly echoing and repeating themselves, but always in a slightly different way, on a different layer of the spiral and at a different stage in time.

Here is an exercise to develop the work we did earlier with the spiral (see p. 69), extending it to include the idea of repetition.

Exercise: 'Starting again'

There are many points in life at which we seem to 'start all over again'. We recognise that we are in some way back at the beginning of a cycle, about to repeat a phase that we know from the past. Yet it is different – it cannot be exactly the same. The person who we are has changed, and time has moved on.

Take an example from my own life: I've run a selling business twice over now. The first time was in my twenties, when I was living in Cambridge, and I began collecting and selling vintage clothes and textiles. After that, I thought I had got the urge to trade out of my system, only to find it resurfacing in my mid-forties, when I started to deal in Russian arts and crafts. In some ways, the pattern was very similar. In both cases, I went to unusual locations to source my stock, then traded informally for several years before taking on shop premises, which I ran both times for five or six years. But each time was different, too. The first business was a very casual affair, which fitted in around the demands of a young family. The second time, I entered a whole new way of life, travelling back and forth to Russia, studying the language and lecturing and writing about Russian traditions as well. The business side too, was more of a commitment, requiring careful stock control, staff management and so on. Both episodes were colourful and exciting, but each brought its own challenges and I learnt different lessons through them.

We all have points that repeat in our lives, cycles which begin all over again. Typical examples might be:

- The birth of another child.
- Embarking on a second or third marriage or major relationship.
- Moving house and settling into a new home.
- Going back to college or taking a new study course.
- Changing direction in your career.

There are likely to be points of repetition too which are unique to you; these could relate to a desire, an urge or a summons from an outside source. Or the precipitating event could be something which apparently comes out of the blue each time, but which, with hindsight, you recognise as something that is similar to a previous experience.

Choose an example of a recurring cycle from your own life, thinking about the similarities and the differences between the repeating phases. Write a short paragraph about it. Then, if you wish, find another couple of examples, and work with them in the same way.

This kind of reflective approach develops over time, and even though I have encouraged you to tackle this exercise straight away, I would also suggest that you keep the idea in mind and see what other insights it may throw up. These can be useful in writing your overall narrative and identifying the patterns there.

In the final chapter too, we will be looking at the bigger picture, and considering the themes that define the storylines of your life.

CHAPTER EIGHT

The Essence of Your Life

O ver eight hundred years ago, singers and poets performed in the courts of southern France, presenting their compositions to the lords and ladies of the castles. They were known as the troubadours, and their songs and verses were chiefly of love. Indeed, they initiated the whole European tradition of what we now call romantic love, which, in their case, usually took the form of an impossible longing for a lady who was out of reach, either married already or beyond their social position. The troubadours were themselves of mixed origin – some of low birth, some dukes in their own right – and their company included a number of women minstrels, properly known as the 'trobaritz'.

Although they sang of pure love, their own lives were often colourful, sometimes even scandalous. It is these lives which are celebrated in a little-known genre called the *vidas*, or 'life stories', of the troubadours. No one is quite sure how these were originally gathered together, but they may have been used to introduce the troubadours' songs and poems after their deaths, either in performance or in written collections of their work. They range from a few lines to a few paragraphs in length, and are remarkable in their frankness, and in their ability to condense a lifetime into a short account. Virtues, faults, crimes, idiosyncrasies and talents are all fair game for inclusion.

> Peire Vidal was from Toulouse. He was the son of a furrier, and he sang better than anyone else in the world. And he was one of the craziest men who ever lived, for he thought that everything that pleased him or that he wished for was real. He invented poetry more easily than anyone else in the world. And he was the one who composed the most beautiful melodies and who told the greatest follies about arms and about love and about slander.

Thus opens the *vida* of one troubadour, and, in the brief account that follows, an amazing number of adventures are packed in. Peire has his tongue cut by a jealous knight when he pretends to be the lover of that knight's wife. Then, recovered from this injury, he travels to Cyprus where he marries a Greek woman who claims to be an heir to the Emperor of Constantinople. Then he loses all his money trying to raise arms to stake a claim to that empire. The story concludes that, despite all evidence to the contrary, he still believes himself 'to be the best knight in the world and the one best loved by the ladies.'

Another troubadour is described as exhibiting 'great girth and great gluttony', while another, a baron of Provence, as a man who in his lifetime 'took pleasure in gifts and gallantry and war and munificence and courts and applause and noise and song and joy'. A further minstrel is given short shrift after his demise, for 'his songs had no great value, nor did he'. Another also had bad performing habits – he was a song-maker from the Perigord who was over-fond of introducing his songs and made his explanation 'longer than the song itself'. (We surely all know people like this today!) He was a romantic soul though, as he pined and died for love after his wife passed away.

From these brief glimpses into the *vidas*, you can see how they were not stiff memorials to the minstrels, but living testimonies to their human qualities – descriptions of the very stuff of their lives, from full-scale dramas to irritating or endearing personal habits. Indeed, they are an early form of the life story, and one that can still be used as a template today.

Life in a Nutshell

Now that we've traced the path to writing a life story through the demands of structure, style and content, and some of the deeper layers of meaning have been added, it's time to finish the journey by contemplating the essence which marks out the uniqueness of each person. At root, who am I? What might people say about me after I am dead and gone? What are my significant characteristics, which could be commemorated in a few short words? What events and actions might I be remembered for?

The *vidas* show one way to approach this, for they seem to capture the personal essence with a wonderful mixture of humour and nobility, the very core of human nature.

In the exercise below, you'll be trying your hand at a *vida*, and your first attempt should be about someone who you knew and who has now passed away. Here is my own *vida* about a dear uncle; as he loved medieval French literature, it seems appropriate that I've chosen him as my subject.

Roy's *vida*

My Uncle Roy was a kind man, who smoked a pipe. His hair was red and his complexion light and freckled. He was a fighter pilot in the Second World War, something of which he would never speak afterwards. He loved the French language, and came to St Andrew's University, where he taught medieval French stories and poems to two generations of students. He could swing a golf club and climb the Pentland Hills. He wrote books, some of them good, some of them unreadable. He was not himself for the last two years of his life, after a stroke, but when he died, we missed him.

I've deliberately taken up some of the *vida* style, which is somewhat medieval in itself, because I think it suits the writing of a 'life in a nutshell'. It's certainly not the only way to do this, but I recommend that you try something along these lines in the first instance.

Exercise: writing a vida

Choose the subject of your *vida*. Take a few minutes to remember the person and the part they played in your life. Jot down a few notes which describe the essence of their life and some of their best-known features, however trivial these might seem. When you are ready, write your *vida* in one to three paragraphs.

Now think about whether you would like to write about yourself in this way. It isn't for everyone, and there is no need to do it if the thought makes you shiver. One woman in my class, however, was deeply touched by the *vidas* that I read out; she said, 'That's the way I'd like to be described when I die'. So do try it, if you want to.

Postcard life stories

Another way to approach the essence of your life is to write it all down on the back of a postcard. American writer, Michael Kimball, has devised his own version of this idea, and offers to write down the life story of any individual, young or old. He sets it down, quite literally, on a postcard (the writing is small, it is true), managing to cram in three hundred words or more. You can find examples, which are both entertaining and inspiring, to read on his website (www.michael-kimball.com/blog.php).

Here's one about a young woman who was finally reunited with her lost love:

Karen Lillis was born on Friday the 13th under a full moon, which led to her being quiet and dark. She moved 7 times by the time she was 7 years old and this made her restless. She didn't want to stay in one place long enough to get hurt. Besides, moving was always hopeful and buoyant. She narrated the receding back window scenery to her baby brother as they travelled across America. In her youth, Karen was conspicuously tall, skinny, and smart. Accordingly, the kids at school taunted her from head to toe, which led to nicknames like Ethiopia, Four

Eyes, and Rex. Because of this, in part, Karen didn't talk in public until about age 15. She escaped the taunting for college and fell in love with Thomas. Their first kiss was at a train station, but they later broke up and he became The One Who Got Away. Karen became obsessed with taking photographs of train tracks and train stations. She may have been looking for Thomas where she last saw him. She felt hopeful when she looked down the train tracks. She thought her future was in the distance. Karen further escaped to NYC, which saved her from being a rag doll or going crazy. Another thing that saved Karen was writing and the cross-country book tour (see moves, above) that she took to support her first book (she's now published three). In NYC, she became irresponsible and preferred affairs to relationships. She wanted people to leave her. It reminded her of Thomas, who she found again – 14 years after they broke up – when he applied to the store where she was working at the time. She asked him to set her free and they got back together a few weeks later. Now they are engaged and living in Pittsburgh, where they are going to stay, at least for a while.

Both the postcard life stories and those of the *vidas* contain little personal details as well as the bigger sweep of events, a combination that really helps to define the individuality of the person and the way that they meet the world. Even if some of these details are foibles, they can convey something of the essence of that person, which is what makes them lovable as a human being. These stories are written by outsiders, of course, which in one way makes it easier to be objective, and in the case of the *vidas*, the passing of time has also helped to distil the story down to its essential components. But even if you cannot emulate these approaches exactly, just reading about them can help to give you a sense of how to go about it, and how to touch the core of truth in relating your own life experiences.

A number of the stories on Michael Kimball's website are a little disturbing too, often reflecting the fragmented nature of many families today, and the difficult backgrounds that some of his subjects have struggled with. (Most do, however, end on an upbeat note, an affirmation which, as suggested earlier, is very important in the setting down of a personal history.) And whatever the story, each one that Michael recounts emphasises the polarities in that person's life – the contrasts of love and rejection, happiness and misery, health and sickness. Rather than smoothing these over, he chooses to express them, and by revealing these dilemmas, he gives the story its impetus, exposing the person's energy and motivation, and the very real challenges that they may still be facing. Unique human endeavour comes from dealing with the oppositions of good and bad, pain and pleasure. It can be tempting in a life story simply to show how you have resolved, forgiven, and transcended hardships, but by doing this you will rub out something of yourself too.

The way we write can also be influenced by the stage of life we have reached. As we move through middle age and beyond, we will tend to reconcile ourselves to what life has brought us and what we have made of it. The process of resolution and integration is a healthy one, and part of growing and maturing as a human being. But in your life story it is still pertinent to ask: what made me grow? What dilemmas did I face?

If you are in your forties or over, try this exercise first, before you do the writing exercise below:

Sit back and relax. Close your eyes, and allow yourself to drift back to a time between your mid-twenties and late thirties when life was challenging for you. What issues did you face? What dilemmas did you have to struggle with? Did this make you grow as a person? Try to remember how raw your feelings may have been, or how impossible a situation was. Then move forward again to the present moment. Allow any agitation to subside. See if you have a different viewpoint, now that you are older and wiser.

Ideally, when you come to write your full narrative, you will be able to include both of these perspectives, so that you bring to life something of the person you were then, as well as the mature and reflective person that you have become. In a way, this is comparable with being both the composer of the *vida* and the troubadour; you have the subjective and the objective viewpoints, represented in this case by the living memories on the one hand, and by the wisdom gained with the passing of time on the other.

You may need to repeat this exercise of going back into the past several times, or allow it to settle over the course of a few days, but when you are satisfied that you have completed it, move on to write your story as suggested below.

Exercise: your life on a postcard

You're now going to write a nutshell version of your life story on a post-card. Try a version in rough first, if you prefer (on paper or on the computer). I suggest aiming at no more than 250 words, although you may need to work to a longer length to start with, then cut down. Next, take a postcard (picture or plain, or even a piece of card cut to the right size if you don't have a postcard to hand) and write your story on the back of it. If your handwriting is really large, use two postcards.

Tips for writing your story in a nutshell:

- Include at least one challenge or dilemma that you have faced.
- Try to say what has motivated or spurred you on.
- Say who or what the most important things in your life have been.
- Look for a storyline that you can weave through this.
- Indicate how things have changed or developed over time.
- Mention one or two habits or idiosyncrasies that you have.
- Don't expect to be able to include everything about yourself or your story.

This might seem a tall order, but most of it will come instinctively, based on the study of the *vidas* and the stories on a postcard. If you can't fit it all in, don't worry. The important thing is to try it out, and to write something of yourself, your character and your life. It can be both inspiring and humbling to see it set down like this.

When the postcard is written, give yourself time to appreciate it. Has it thrown up any burning issues which you haven't managed to include here? If so, note them down and see if you can weave them into your main life story narrative. Then put the postcard away for a week or so, before reviewing it. Does it surprise you, to see your life written in such a succinct way? Does it give you ideas about how you would like your life to develop in future? After all, writing your life story is not just about producing your narrative, but also about contemplating your life's journey and finding fresh inspiration for the road ahead.

Choosing a motto

'Where there's a will, there's a way'; 'Life is not just a rehearsal'; 'Better late than never'; 'Love conquers all'; 'Live as if you had a thousand years; act as though you are going to die tomorrow' . . .

Do you have a favourite motto or proverb? Now that we've got to the heart of the life story, you might like to choose one that reflects your aspirations and your outlook on life. Give yourself time to make the choice; I suggest that you write down any that occur to you now, and look out for any others that may come your way over the next few weeks. You can use a simple Internet search to help you. As well as the old favourites from the English language, there are some very beautiful and unusual ones to be found in other cultures as well, such as this Cherokee Indian expression: 'When you were born, you cried and the world rejoiced. Live your life so that when you die, the world cries and you rejoice.' (I found this one, which struck me in particular, on www.inspirationalspark.com.)

Try your chosen motto (or mottos – there can be more than one) out for size. Sure, they are only sayings, but they've been rolled around like pebbles in a stream, and the common ones have been smoothed and polished by the force of popular use. What do they say – or not say – in relation to your life and about you as a person?

Mottos can be used in your life story if you wish. A motto quoted on the opening page makes a good prelude, or you could insert one at the start of each chapter or section of your story. You may also find a point in the narrative where you can use such a saying to explain your outlook, or why you took the path that you did. However, it is not essential to put these into your life story at all; you could just use them to help you define your own motivation and purpose, and this will, in any case, be an aid to focusing your writing.

Drawing Conclusions: The Story That Never Ends

You will always find more that isn't encapsulated in a motto, a life story on a postcard, or a blueprint life story. Ask yourself what that is, and whether you can find a way of including it in your narrative. Perhaps it is a characteristic which you have ignored up till now, or an event which has significance but which you haven't written about – maybe it didn't seem important before, but you can now see how it has affected or influenced you.

But bear in mind a saying often quoted by my own mentor: 'There is always further to go.' In one sense, there is never a final resting point. The chances are that you will never finish recording all your memories or defining yourself fully as a person, even though you will produce a wonderful narrative or life memoir. As long as you go on living and breathing, you have the chance to discover more, to know yourself better and to become more receptive to the miracle of life itself. The pilgrimage continues.

The Spindle of Life: Fortune, Fate, Destiny and Necessity

There is an old Greek story about the spindle that turns at the centre of the universe. It is known as the Spindle of Necessity, and is turned by the Goddess of Necessity with the aid of her daughters, the three Fates. Is this idea relevant to our own lives? Are we subject to ruling powers such as these, which govern the way in which our story is played out?

There may not be any simple answers to these questions, and as most traditions of wisdom indicate, our lives are most probably a mixture of free will and of dictates beyond our immediate control. However, the creative element of individual life – the way in which we fulfil our potential and leave a mark – may come about as a result of how we handle these two aspects of human existence. We are neither pre-ordained, nor totally at liberty. And the interaction between gods and humans, as the ancient Greeks saw it, is what makes for an 'interesting' life.

Taking the myth a little further, the goddess and the three Fates can be seen in a different role, as four powers of life, each affecting us in its own way. The mother – the Spindle – is the power of Necessity lying at the heart of existence; her daughters, the three Fates, can be seen in different but interconnected roles, each representing one of the ruling forces that shape individual circumstance. In this interpretation they are known as Fortune, Fate and Destiny.

To round off this book, I am going to explore the meaning of these four terms: Fortune, Fate, Destiny and Necessity, perhaps to inspire you to take the ideas further, and to include something of them in your life story if you wish. They may not feel immediately familiar or relevant, so I suggest taking them on board for now, and seeing if they begin to yield insights over the course of writing your story.

Fortune

The Goddess of Fortune turns her wheel; it rises up and down, circling round and round for ever. This image, probably originating in Roman mythology, has been absorbed into Western culture too, symbolising the rise and fall of the fortunes of individuals, families and nations.

Fortune is what is commonly called 'luck'. It is what comes your way 'by chance', but because certain types of event keep arising, you may recognise it as more than chance. For instance, I am often lucky in finding exactly the book I need at the right moment. I am not lucky in prize draws or competitions. What kind of luck do you have? What are you habitually lucky or unlucky with?

Then there are single events or circumstances which are often described as lucky or otherwise. 'We were lucky with the weather.' 'It was unfortunate that the car was pulling out just as I came round the bend.' 'I'm lucky to have you.' 'It was a bit of bad luck, losing my necklace.' What events in recent months would you ascribe to good or bad luck? Are there any key happenings in your lifetime which you feel were due to this?

What are your own views on luck? The questions below may help you to get below the surface and dig out your own thoughts and feelings on it. Once again, there is no one right answer here, but if you give full weight and consideration to the questions, you may discover more about the nature of fortune in your own life.

Do you think luck is caused by:

- Your genetic inheritance?
- Forces beyond your control?
- Individual personality?
- The moment at which you were born?
- Coincidence?
- Spiritual intervention?
- Willpower?
- Any or all of the above?
- None of the above – it's an illusion?

Fate

Returning to the old Greek myth, fate can be seen as the spinning, measuring and cutting of a thread. 'When your time's up, it's up.' 'They were fated to meet.' 'A fate worse than death.' These are more common types of expression which convey the power of fate to terminate one phase and to initiate another. There is a tendency to think of fate as 'bad' – an unexpected and unwelcome turn of events – but this may not be entirely so. Some teachings suggest that while you can go blindly with your fate, seeing and knowing nothing, you also have the choice to wake up, to embrace it and thus to align yourself with the greater life of the universe that produced you. Or, as the teachings also suggest, sometimes by being awake in the moment, you may be able to step away from a pull of fate, not giving in to its tugs. In so doing, you may achieve more freedom to serve life and fulfil your destiny. Deciding whether to go with your fate, or whether to avoid it on any given occasion can be one of the hardest choices a person has to make (Hamlet, perhaps?), but it is also the mark of a human being with great insight and strength of purpose.

Fate can seem ambiguous; it's a difficult topic, with a number of different takes on it. But if you wrestle with it a little, you may find that it is both enlightening and less threatening than it first appears. Fate is a little like the Grey Wolf in the Russian fairy tale 'Prince Ivan and the Firebird'. Grey Wolf first confronts the prince in a ferocious manner, killing and eating his horse. But then he turns into a faithful guide who accompanies the prince on his travels, warns him of danger and saves him, ultimately, from death itself. So try not to be too hasty in condemning fate or in dismissing the concept altogether.

Try out the following questions in order to explore your own experiences of fate, and your views on it:

- Do you believe in fate?
- Can you think of any occurrences of fate in your own life?
- Did it change things for better or for worse?
- Can you avoid fate or make other choices?

Destiny

Destiny and fate are words that are too often used interchangeably. But although dictionaries may suggest overlapping meanings, they also define them with differing characteristics. According to *Chambers Dictionary* (1997), for example, the word 'destiny' comes from the Latin verb *stare*, meaning to stand, and is 'the purpose or end to which any person or thing is appointed'; the original meaning of the word 'fate', however, is 'a prediction'.

So here you have the idea of a destiny that is given to you, a role you have been granted in life. But, like any job offer, the appointment is not always taken up. There may be a choice as to whether you take on your proffered destiny or not. Likewise, even if you do step into the shoes of destiny, as it were, you may wander around, on and off the track, for a long time until you really begin to fulfil it.

Circumstances may also play a part, and perhaps destiny is a combination of individual potential and the events and environment that surround you. It is a common perception that Winston Churchill was 'destined' to lead Britain to victory in the Second World War, but obviously there had to be a war for that to happen. Destiny is often 'bigger' than the individual, so that it is accompanied by a sense of that person having to grow to fill a role, or prove themselves capable of taking on a task requiring great strength or ability.

You may not currently be aware of destiny playing a part in your life, but by exploring this idea, you may begin to find ways in which it has meaning for you, and perhaps see how it governs some of your actions. Consider the following questions:

- Which famous people do you think fulfilled their destiny?
- Was it their individual nature or circumstance that brought this about?
- Do you think destiny has played a role in your own life?
- What do you think your destiny is, or could be?

Necessity

The final one of the four powers brings us back to the image of the Spindle of Necessity, the axis that turns at the centre of life, and without which there would be no individual lives, no action, no evolution or time passing. You may be able to channel your fortune, to some extent, deal with fate, step into your destiny, but in the face of necessity you can only choose to act on it, or not – and that choice may not always be available.

There are, in fact, relatively few moments in life when it is absolutely necessary to do something, but when those moments are recognised, and acted on, there is a clarity of purpose where argument, egotism and personal sensitivities have no place. You do what you have to do. You step out of your normal frame of reference, aligning yourself with the necessity of the moment. It may happen that you snatch a child who is tottering on a cliff top without a second's hesitation, or that you suddenly know with complete certainty that you have to walk away from a relationship. You might, on another occasion, have to drop everything to go to the bedside of a relative who is dying.

Necessity, like destiny, gives you the sense of something impersonal and far greater than your own individual life. You cannot live at the level of necessity all the time; even though you can acknowledge its existence, you spend most of the time in the everyday world of interactions, thoughts and minor happenings. But every now and then, there may be nothing standing between you and necessity, and then you may act in accordance with its pure nature. Certainly, childbirth was one such experience for me, as I expect it is for many women, yielding to the overpowering necessity of giving birth, which felt more 'real' than anything in my life beforehand. Possibly any man who has fought in a war will also know the force of necessity, and how it can demand a response and govern actions taken.

Reflect on the following questions, and if you don't have an immediate response, let them simmer away for a while and see if they produce any answers later on:

- Can you think of any moments in your life when 'necessity' has taken over?
- What was the nature of your response? How did you act?
- What were the consequences?

Tip:
When you recognise a moment of 'necessity' that has occurred in your life, write a paragraph or two about the occasion and how it affected you. Be as clear and as accurate as possible about what happened.

Writing Luck into Your Life

The concepts we've just covered are deep and philosophical ones, and can be hard to grapple with immediately. When I first came across them, I was, if the truth be told, rather suspicious of them, and felt that they were too abstract. However, I allowed them a little room in my mental framework, and after a while I began to see how they do, in fact, provide a real guide to the nature of different types of experience. I would therefore recommend that you give them some thought, then leave them to find their own place in your outlook. Write them into your narrative if you wish to, or leave them to simmer on the back burner, where they may act in a potent way, crystallising the threads of meaning in your story.

Conclusion

This just leaves me to pick up the theme of luck again, and to wish you the very best of it with writing your own life story! I hope that your journey will be both stimulating and fulfilling, and that the task you are undertaking will enhance your own life path, as well as creating a precious narrative for your family and friends. May your own life story be a bright star, shining with inspiration for those who read it.

Life Story Writing Checklist

This checklist can be used both to make sure that you are following the main principles when writing your narrative, and also as a handy at-a-glance guide to the chapter in which they're discussed.

THEME	CHAPTER
1. Planning your story	
Setting up the structure for your life story in sections or chapters	6
Preparing a chronology of the key events and phases of your life	2, 6
Choosing a form to present your story	2
Thinking up a title	4
2. Gathering and selecting material	
Finding types of material and items to include	2
Using prompts to recover memories	3
Exploring the senses to bring back memories	3
Keeping notes as you go along	6
Honing down your material	4

7. Reading, checking, and adding finishing touches

8. Exercises for insight and imagination

9. General resources

In the Resources section, you will find book, Internet, and archive listings for help with writing technique, life story presentation, historical background, professional services, life story printing and production and family history research.

Resources

This section includes both books and Internet resources, and they are divided according to the particular use they may have. There is also a section on family history, for those who would like to research this further with a view to including aspects of it in their life story.

Many of the resources given here are either international or accessible worldwide. In other cases, pointers are given as to how they may be located for particular regions.

All resources have been checked as far as possible, and were accurate at the time of going to press.

Note: please see p. 26 for notes on Internet safety.

Life Story Writing and Tuition

Cherry Gilchrist offers online/correspondence courses, consultancy and class tuition. She may also be available for writing and editing commissions. Please see her dedicated website at www.write4life.com. Further details of her work can be viewed at www.cherrygilchrist. co.uk.

Other classes may be found by checking study centres, local authority classes, part-time college courses and independent organisations in your area. (A couple of sample websites for courses and classes are listed below, under general Internet resources.)

Books

Writing your life story

Barrington, Judith, *Writing a Memoir* (Eight Mountain Press, Oregon, USA, 2004). An excellent, thoughtful study, with useful exercises, which are helpful for life stories as well as memoirs.

Daniel, Lois, *How to Write Your Own Life Story* (Chicago Review Press, Chicago, 1997). Includes many examples taken from life stories written by her students; less useful for technique.

Heffron, Jack, *The Writer's Idea Book* (Writer's Digest Books, Ohio, USA, 2000). Contains mostly 'prompts' for writing ideas which could be useful for life stories.

Marshall, Carl and David, *The Book of Myself*: *A do-it-yourself autobiography in 201 questions* (Hyperion, USA, 1994). This is simply a 201-page book with a question at the top of each page, and the rest left blank for you to fill in. Could be enjoyable as a workbook, or as a notebook for collating your memories en route to writing your life story.

Neubauer, Joan R., *From Memories to Manuscript*: *The Five-Step Method of Writing Your Life Story* (Myfamily.com.inc, Utah, USA, 2002). A short but useful book, with a no-nonsense approach.

Oke, Michael, *Write Your Own Life Story* (How To Books, UK, 2004) and *Write Your Life Story* (How To Books, UK, 2008). These two editions differ significantly from each other. The first is an enjoyable book of 'prompts', with triggers for each phase of life and different decades of UK history, plus examples from people's life stories; the second focuses more on the 'how to' aspects of actually writing your story, with guidance for producing your own life story book.

Rainer, Tristine, *Your Life as Story* (Penguin Putnam, New York, 1998). A more elaborate study, useful for literary writing guidelines and for less ambitious writers to dip into for ideas.

Creative writing and life writing

There are many books on creative writing in general. This list is by no means exhaustive, but suggests titles which might be useful in the context of life story writing, or to take your writing further.

Adams, Kathleen, *Journal to the Self*: *Twenty-Two Paths to Personal Growth* (Grand Central Publishing, USA, 1990). A course in journal writing, with the intention of encouraging self-development.

Anderson, Linda (ed.), *Creative Writing: A Workbook with Readings* (published for the Open University by Routledge, Oxfordshire, 2006). An excellent resource book with clear suggestions, examples from literature and a good section on life writing. Aimed more at the creative writing student overall, but plenty of useful tips for the life story too.

Birch, Cathy, *Awaken the Writer Within* (How To Books, Oxford, UK, 2005). Suggests exercises for creative writing, which also include imaginative use of dreams and Tarot cards.

Roorbach, Bill, *Writing Life Stories* (Story Press, Ohio, USA, 1998). A more literary survey of biography/memoir with analysis of various texts, plus accounts of teaching life writing.

Life story source books

Hallowell, Dr Edward, *Human Moments: How to find meaning and love in your everyday life* (Thorsons, London, 2002). The author recounts moments that have touched his life, many taken from the experiences of other people who have talked to him.

Isay, Dave, *Listening is an Act of Love* (Penguin, USA, 2007). A fascinating anthology of life story extracts, taken from the unique Story Corps project in the USA. 'Story booths' set up in different parts of the country are visited by ordinary people who come in pairs to record (in audio form) their life stories. More than ten thousand pairs have made recordings to date.

Facer, Sian (ed.), *On This Day: The History of the World in 366 Days* (Octopus Publishing, 1992). Divided into a page for each day of the year, with records of world events associated with that date.

Reilly, Carmel, *The Day My Life Changed* (Magpie Books, London, 2006). An excellent collection of international first-hand narratives about life-changing experiences, grouped by theme. (See p. 156 for an example.)

Yesterday's Britain: The illustrated story of how we lived, worked and played in this century (Reader's Digest, London, 1998). Coverage of the twentieth century by period, with good illustrations, key events, social history and a useful timeline.

Autobiographies and memoirs

There are innumerable autobiographies available, and you will find your own favourites – here are some that have 'spoken' to me in recent years, and which I have found inspirational for my own writing:

W. H. Davies, *The Autobiography of a Supertramp* (1908, reprint editions are available).

Frame, Janet, *The Envoy From Mirror City* (HarperCollins, London, 1993: original edition 1984). The third part of an autobiography by a famous New Zealand author, whose originality and vision was hampered by mental problems and a struggle to be accepted in the modern world.

Fraser, Eugenie, *The House by the Dvina: A Russian Childhood* (Corgi, UK, 1997). A warm, evocative account of a Scottish girl growing up in pre-revolutionary Russia.

Mantel, Hilary, *Giving Up the Ghost* (Fourth Estate, London, 2003). The childhood section of this memoir is remarkable for its recall of a child's perception of the world.

Historical interest

These are all examples of life stories and memoirs set down in previous centuries, ranging from those about the poorest in the land to anecdotes about more illustrious members of society.

Aubrey, John, *Brief Lives* (various editions). Life histories collected by Aubrey in the seventeenth century, involving reminiscences, historical information, scandal and rumour! Subjects include Dr John Dee and Sir Walter Raleigh.

Koa Wing, Sandra (ed.), *Our Longest Days: A People's History of the Second World War* (Profile Books, London, 2008). Verbatim accounts from volunteers who undertook to keep a personal journal for the Mass Observation project.

Mayhew, Henry, *Mayhew's Characters* and *London's Underworld* (various editions). Published from 1851 to 1862, these are extraordinary 'life stories' of the poor and dispossessed of London's streets, collected by Mayhew.

Samuel Pepys, The Diaries of (various editions). Pepys kept diaries not intended for public consumption, but they have provided us with racy personal accounts that are also illuminating about life at the time.

The Vidas *of the Troubadours*, Garland Library of Medieval Literature, vol. 6, series B (Garland Publishing Inc., New York & London, 1984). Remarkable medieval life stories of minstrels, distilled from their colourful lives.

Internet Resources for Life Stories

There is an ever-growing number of websites offering a variety of aids for life story writing. Here are just a few examples; by using search engines you will find many more.

Creating your life story online:
www.meremembered.com

Inspirational mottos and sayings (see pp. 178–179):
www.inspirationalspark.com/index.html

Life stories on a postcard:
www.michael-kimball.com/blog.php

Create a timeline in Microsoft Excel:
www.vertex42.com/ExcelArticles/timeline.html

Story Works – courses in life story writing in Australia:
www.storyworks.com.au

STT courses:
www.sttcourses.co.uk
A long-established British school of writing courses which includes a certificate in life story writing.

For world events and history that you've lived through:
www.datesinhistory. com; traditionsonwheels.org;
and history1900s.about. com.

Sound archives on the Internet

British Library Sound Archive: www.sounds.bl.uk/. Listen (free) to a
multitude of oral-history recordings, including the memories of
Holocaust survivors, artists and jazz musicians.

Story Corps, USA: www.storycorps.org/. Extracts from the thousands of
life stories recorded nationwide are posted on this website, which is
continually updated.

Help with Life Story Publishing

If you would like to have your life story written and published in book
form, there are several companies who specialise in this enterprise.
Some will complete the whole process for you; they conduct personal
interviews to gather your memories, write the story for you, and design
and print the final book. Others may mentor you while you write, then
produce the book for you.

Be aware that this process does not come cheap, as many hours
of professional expertise are involved.

Note: all the companies listed here are reputable to the best of the
author's knowledge, but no personal responsibility can be taken for
any claims made by them or for the quality of their work.

Biograph: 17 Ramsey Road, Warboys, Cambridgeshire, PE28 2RW;
telephone 01487 824016; www.biograph.co.uk

The Book of My Life: 2nd floor, 145–157 St John Street, London, EC1V
4PY; telephone 0845 643 9423; www.bookofmylife.co.uk.

Bound Biographies: Michael Oke & Associates, Heyford Park House, Heyford Park, Bicester, OX25 5HD; telephone 01869 232911; www.boundbiographies. com.

Memoir Publishing: Louise Millar & Associates, telephone 07790 902083; email enquiries@memoirpublishing.com; www.memoirpublishing. com.

Lifeline ink: www.lifelineink.co.uk

VANITY PUBLISHING

Beware of 'vanity publishing' firms, who will charge you dear for producing your book and offering some kind of distribution deal. They may flatter you, and imply that your memoir is suitable for a wider market, which is highly unlikely to be the case. Very few people, professional authors included, will ever produce a personal biography that will be accepted for normal commercial publication.

Neither the companies who offer to help you write and produce your life story, nor the print-on-demand publishers (see p. 198), will make any such claims. Nor will they usually distribute your work for you. The end product of their services is the printed edition of your story.

Self-Publishing Your Life Story

You can also print your own life story (see pp. 37–38). There are publishers who specialise in what is known as 'print-on-demand', and can supply as small or as large a number of books as you like. (The greater the quantity, the cheaper the price per copy.) The book must be submitted electronically, e.g. in PDF or Word form, and can be stored electronically for future print runs. It's usually possible to include almost any number of black and white photos or illustrations, though these will be reproduced on the page, so the quality won't be as good as photographic plates.

At the present time, with many print-on-demand publishers, although covers can be full colour, there is no easy way to include colour pictures economically in the text. But more innovative companies, especially those operating chiefly on the internet, are now finding ways to include colour images at a cost that is affordable for printing a few special copies, if not for wider circulation.

Self-publishing is unlikely to be commercially viable unless you have a ready market for your memoirs – for instance, if you often give talks and can sell copies to the audience. However, it's an excellent way of producing your life story to high standards, and having bound copies to pass on to friends and family. You will need to contact print-on-demand publishers individually to find out their terms and what services they offer, such as whether they will produce a cover design for you if you are unable to supply your own. Do your costings carefully, and remember that you can always order more copies later, rather than ending up with boxes of books under the bed!

More and more publishers are offering print-on-demand, so it's impossible to give a comprehensive listing here. Try local telephone directories or do a national Internet search. Here are three of the major companies in the field:

Antony Rowe: (head office) Bumper's Farm, Chippenham, Wiltshire, SN14 6LH; telephone 01249 659705; www.antonyrowe.co.uk. A well-established and reliable company known for producing good-quality volumes and offering transparent quotes for the costs. It's not necessary to live nearby to use this company.

Lulu: An online company that has been a popular choice in recent years for all kinds of self-publishing, including photo books, hard-backs and paperbacks, and various other types of format. Colour images can be included. See their website for latest details: www.lulu.com/uk

Blurb: This company has easy-to-use software which you can down-load from the Internet, and then design your own life story book at your leisure, using colour photos as well if you wish. You can print out and proof your book, then upload the finished result, and order printed copies directly from the company. Production quality is excellent. The finished costs, including postage from the USA, put it on a par with an expensive specialist illustrated book, so most people would probably only order a few copies. www.blurb.com

Life Story Templates

It's possible to find or buy templates on the Internet, which you can use to create your life story. Be aware that many come from the USA, so that if you live in the UK or elsewhere this will affect any shipping costs, and also the wording and product may be created using American style. Life story writing is already extremely popular in the States. Try a search such as 'life story template', 'memory book' or 'digital scrapbook'.

The major family history website, www.ancestry.co.uk also has a link to its publishing arm, 'Canvas', where you can create a family history book, which might also be suitable for a life story.

There is a simple life story template available free through Microsoft Office online as a Powerpoint download.

Family History

Books

There are dozens of books on the subject, and if you live outside the UK, you will probably wish to track down some which are more specific to your region. You can do this through major online booksellers or through family history websites. Otherwise, bookshops and libraries are the places to ask for advice.

When buying family history books, do check the date of the edition you are using, especially if buying second hand. If you plan to do much of your research online, for instance, it's essential to have good, up-to-date information about Internet resources and using websites. If you are going to approach it through archives and books, then older versions from ten or fifteen years ago may still be very handy, as not much will have changed during that period.

Barratt, Nick, *Who Do You Think You Are? Encyclopaedia of Genealogy* (Harper, UK, 2008). Associated with the popular television series of the same name, this attractively presented book sets out to make the first and intermediate steps in family-history research clear and enjoyable.

Herber, Mark D., *Ancestral Trails: The Complete Guide to British Genealogy and Family History* (History Press, UK, 2008). A substantial tome, which has a place on the bookshelf of a serious researcher, but is probably more for reference than for reading straight through. Respected as a classic guide in its field. Look for the most recent version that you can find.

Rogers, Colin D., *The Family Tree Detective: A Manual for Tracing Your Ancestors in England and Wales* (Manchester University Press, UK, 4th revised edition, 2008). A useful and comprehensive guide to research, which has become a standard reference book.

Magazines

These can often be found at newsagents or ordered by subscription, and they are a good source of articles and information that will give you ideas for research and of the latest resources available. Among those currently published in the UK are, *Your Family History*, *Who Do You Think You Are?* and *Your Family Tree*.

Websites

There are a multitude of family history websites, and once you begin research, you will quickly find your way to others. Family history magazines are a good source of updates, and of indicating websites for very specific genealogy interests.

Ancestry: www.ancestry.co.uk. The best known of the genealogy websites, providing a large international database of census and birth, marriage and death information, plus a wealth of extras such as telephone books, passenger shipping lists and electoral rolls. It also has facilities for uploading your tree, so you may be able to make contact with other people whose trees link to yours. Subscription based; some free search facilities available.

Cyndi's List: www.cyndislist.com/. Lists a huge variety of family history websites covering many different countries. Frequently updated. Free.

Family Search: www.familysearch.org. A remarkable resource created by the Church of Latter-Day Saints, who have carefully transcribed genealogy records from many different countries. A large number are available online, and many more can be ordered for viewing at your local Family Search centre, which you can locate through the website. Free.

Find My Past: www.findmypast.com. Another well-established and reasonably comprehensive website, with many extra resources. Subscription based; some free search facilities available.

Genuki: www.genuki.org.uk. A compendium of genealogical information, chiefly for the British Isles, relating mainly to places and surnames. Free.

The National Archives: www.nationalarchives.gov.uk. Well worth checking for a mention of your ancestors through a general search, or for more specific military, judicial and civilian documents relating to them. It can also direct you to records held at regional UK archives. Free, with payment facilities for downloads of documents, where available.

Index

(Bold type signifies illustrations/diagrams)